KNEE DEEP:
A 9-Month Whirlpool of Handwritten Letters to the Creator

Christina M. Eder

Felicity Press

Copyright © 2021 by Christina M. Eder

Cover by Red Paint Spilman
Interior layout by Rita M. Reali

Writer's Prayer by Sarah Hamaker Used with permission. Copyright by Sarah Hamaker. This prayer appeared in *Prayers for Writers,* a compilation from Capital Christian Writers Fellowship, ccwritersfellowship.org.

No portion of this book may be reproduced in any form or by any means, including electronic storage and retrieval systems, without the expressed prior written permission of the author.

Connect with Christina on Facebook (www.facebook.com/EDERAuthor).

Eder, Christina M.
KNEE DEEP: A 9-Month Whirlpool of Handwritten Letters to the Creator

ISBNs:
978-1-7346596-2-7 (paperback)
978-1-7346596-3-4 (ebook)

Printed in the U.S.A.
First American edition, May 2021

Other books by Christina M. Eder:

Life's Too Short for Dull Razors, Cheap Pens, and Worn Out Underwear

The FROG Blog: Learning on a Lily Pad

UNTHAWED: Lessons from a Frozen Lily Pad

Back Story of *KNEE DEEP: A 9-Month Whirlpool of Handwritten Letters to the Creator*

This book has required deeper knee bends than I have ever experienced. In keeping nine months of handwritten letters to God, I've been on my knees. Knees for praying, bowing in humility, shaking from "wows" and "ows." I've even had a few moments where something so hilarious has taken me to my knees from laughing so hard.

Other than myself, my husband or roles people have played in this journey, I have omitted most names. In reflecting about who and what shaped this book, I realized I would need an additional dozen pages to give credit where credit is due.

My leading cast member in the FROG Blog is God. Some people refer to Jesus, Holy Spirit, Creator, Jehovah, Lord, Higher Power, Father, Abba. The list goes on. You'll see various titles I have used to address my Creator. For simplicity's sake, I choose to use God as my universal reference. We all have belief and rely on something. From gravity to support us to car brakes to protect us, I believe and rely on God as one source for all needs.

I discovered how each handwritten letter showcases the value of one. One person, one word, one sentence, one situation, one online resource. Each one could be included in a rolling credit at the end of this literary film.

I thank each person for who they are.

I'm grateful for every situation. Some people and circumstances have been helpful, some seemed harmful at the time. I've sailed new waters on life's lily pad via dream boats and hardships. Each one has taught, shaped and developed my story.

Perhaps one of my readers will wonder if an unnamed person is him/her. Maybe someone has specific questions or input about a letter. Feedback gives me food for thought. My contemplative nature welcomes a challenge (delivered in love or to listen-to-understand).

You may follow or subscribe to my FROG Blog at www.gueststarcoaching.com. I post weekly messages on my Facebook page, as Christina M. Eder-Author.

If you feel led to follow up on any part of *Knee Deep: A 9-month Whirlpool of Handwritten Letters to the Creator*, I invite you to take that leap of faith. I spend ample time on a computer and gladly welcome any non-screen communication. Feel free to drop me a card at:

Christina M. Eder
P.O. Box 5181
Oak Ridge, TN 37830

Introduction

Posted over a period of three weeks on the FROG Blog and my Facebook author page during the month of March 2020

Zowie!

Professionally speaking, "zowie" isn't a preferred word to summarize this twist in the FROG Blog book series. However, zowie is the only word I muster to describe a jaw-dropping "I-didn't-expect-this-variation-in-my-writing-schedule-and-now-how-on-earth-am-I-going-to-modify-my-plans?" experience. How can I take this sharp fork in the road and not have it feel like a knife in my spleen?

I pause long enough to come up for air and breathe. *Zowie.*

I invite you to enter swirling waters with me as I adapt to the current evolution of these FROG Blog books:

The FROG Blog began in 2017, during a phase when I felt a sense of internal decay. Unexplained restlessness had become a heavy weight. I hit a temporary face-off with anxiety-laden paralysis. I needed to move my courage muscles and realized the only way to strengthen any muscles was to use them.

I read Eleanor Roosevelt's quote, "When you look fear in the face, you are able to say to yourself, 'I lived through this horror. I can take the next thing that comes along.' We must do that which we think we cannot."

Newly inspired, I challenged myself to face the summer of 2017 with one daily act of courage. At the time, confidence was an *act* because I certainly wasn't feeling bold or brave.

(Spoiler alert: if you saw my courageous acts list from that summer, some may consider them child's play. For my then-chaotic soul, each valiant practice became an act of heroism).

In a future post, I may invite readers to request my "Summer Life as Eleanor Roosevelt Would Live" list. For now, this first installment of candidness will suffice as a down payment.

> *After a few days of calling the act "my scary for the day," I realized I was feeding the beast I was trying to starve.*

Originally, I had referred to my summer Eleanor Roosevelt Project as "Doing one scary thing every day." After a few days of calling the act "my scary for the day," I realized I was feeding the beast I was trying to starve. So I released that trap by redefining "scary" to "adventure."

One result from my Eleanor Roosevelt Adventures was hiring someone to establish a website for the FROG Blog. Thanks to a little gal who told me what her FROG bracelet stood for (an acronym for Fully Rely On God), FROG Blog seemed catchy to me and it served as a reminder of my commitment to my Creator.

The FROG Blog launched from my writing studio in 2017 and I took a lunge of courage to jump onto an unclaimed lily pad. That summer, it seemed everywhere I looked, frogs appeared in numerous ways, as if reassuring me I was on the right track.

I was still working on *Life's Too Short for Dull Razors, Cheap Pens, and Worn-Out Underwear,* a project generated by Allisa, my friend since we were four years old. In 2008, she had double-dog dared me to write a book about what I thought about while I run. Eight years later – sometimes one sentence at a time – I finished *Life's Too Short for Dull Razors, Cheap Pens, and Worn-Out Underwear.* I hadn't titled the book yet. I finished it as a tongue-in-cheek volley back to Allisa's dare, so I wanted the title to be whimsical. It only made sense to have it published on April Fool's Day.

Fast forward through a lengthy and tedious process. *Life's Too Short for Dull Razors, Cheap Pens, and Worn-Out Underwear* debuted April 1, 2018. Thinking the book was my "one and done," I was shocked when Chris, my publisher, asked when the next *Life's Too Short* book in the series would be completed. What? Series? Another book?

Thinking he was simply returning my April Fool's joke, I laughed.

Speed through 30 minutes of publisher-author dialogue...

Chris suggested modeling my website FROG Blog posts to create a book series of FROG stories. Gulp for air.

Fast forward through another year of endurance on a lightning-pace project, which included 23 other people each writing their own FROG story...

FROG Blog: Learning on a Lily Pad, the first of a five-book series, was published in May 2019. The second book is on my layout/editor's desk. *UNTHAWED: Lessons From a Frozen Lily Pad* is targeted to launch Spring 2020.

I'm on a three-year schedule to complete my remaining three FROG books. This is where Zowie trumpets its grand entrance in this "adventure."

According to my (emphasis on *my*, ahem) plan, book #3 of the five is a children's version of FROGs called *TADPOLES: Lessons from a Tiny Lily Pad.* #4 is *POETRY POD: Free-Spirited Living on a Lily Pad.* And #5 is *KNEE DEEP,* yet to have its subtitle.

I *planned* to work up enough courage to write *KNEE DEEP* (the most vulnerable piece) last. I figured 2022 would allow time for my faith to catch up with action. I wanted to save that "last" book for when I had more book sales, more reviews, more trust, more followers, more... yes, courage.

Then I received some "out-of-this-world" direction and it seems my Eleanor Roosevelt Project has taken a vacation. I am to write *KNEE DEEP,* not *TADPOLES,* while waiting for *UNTHAWED* to publish. Zowie.

In October 2019, I began a nine-month writing quest. I started handwriting a series of short letters to God because I wanted to do something unique to recognize my pregnancy with our son 30 years ago.

Those letters are meant to be reviewed after this nine-month venture. I'll plan a retreat after July 16, 2020, our son's thirtieth birthday, to reflect on whatever lessons develop during this, my "literary pregnancy."

I've written daily Creator Chats since October and immediately file each letter in a chronologically ordered accordion folder. I stash the letters quickly to avoid my tendency to review, edit, judge or – for some chats – take to the Dumpster. I'd always thought it'd be neat to publish a short, handwritten diary, so I planned to write *KNEE DEEP* from pieces of my 2019 to 2022 journals. I planned to copy the entries that related to the three-year journey of a newly published author. I had planned to handwrite them and print a small book diary. Plans. Plans. Plans. There's an old saying: "We plan, God laughs." I set off in that direction and that's where Divine guidance intersected with Zowie.

"Zowie guidance" indicated that instead of writing pieces from my 2019-2021 journals, I would be using my God talks from this nine-month reflection as a launch pad for my *Knee Deep* book. Thus, *Knee Deep* is to be published before either *Tadpoles* or *Poetry Pod*.

A paraphrased inner response from my "Zowie guidance"...

What? You mean some of my Creator Chats may potentially be printed? For the world to access? For the general public to read? To be viewed by most people who don't even know me? Lord! In no way have I begun this reflective nine-month expedition with the intent to have some of my Creator Chats published!

You know some of those letters contain insights too powerful for me to comprehend right now. Some of these recent sucker punches are too painful to process. Some Creator Chats are so mundane I could use them as a sleep aid – but not to publish!

God, it's one thing to practice courage. It's another thing to be courageously wise. I think You've developed enough wisdom in me to refrain from foolishly opening our conversations to possibly guide others! I don't want people to read me like a book, pun intended. Zowie!

However, I need to live in the here and now. If I am to honor my Creator and live what FROG represents (Fully Rely on God), then I need to say yes and fulfill my promise. I hear the now. I shudder. I don't know the later. I shudder at the thought of later. Zowie.

Sometime after July 16, 2020, I trust I will review this literary time capsule of conversations with God. For now, I know whatever transpires between here and now and there and then will become part of *KNEE DEEP*.

For now, I know I am to continue handwriting daily Creator Chats and immediately file the letters chronologically in an accordion file (before rereading, before editing). For now, I know nearly each letter begins with Thank You. For now, I know both the *TADPOLES* and *POETRY POD* projects will be resting on the FROG's lily pad until 2021.

For now, I know I fiercely question this guidance, yet I'm resolved. I know, for now, I'm to continue our chats from the natural, undiluted flow of my heart. And I am to write for my Audience of One.

For now, I know I struggle to avoid the temptation to filter my Creator Chats. For now, I know I fear He'll later ask me to write and publish parts of our conversations.

There are more zowie moments from this project realignment. Those details may be a story for later. For now, I breathe deeply to post online what will come later.

One word. Zowie.

Note to Myself

Dear Self,

   Write the book that needs to be written. Write even if you and God are the only readers. Write the book that is hardest to write. Some day you could use your journals to write a book.

   Don't worry about publishing. And don't be concerned with the end. Do not fear the messy broken pieces it takes to complete a whole manuscript. Consider these turns of your literary creation as colored chips in your life's kaleidoscope.

Eighteen positive online reviews hardly warranted writing a third book. And yet. And yet. And yet.

   Marjorie Holmes gained national following with her book, <u>I've Got to Talk to Somebody, God: A Woman's Conversations with God</u>. She considered this book a collection of her apron-pocket prayers. Then there's <u>The Diary of a Young Girl</u> by Anne Frank. Thousands of memoirs like these have gone before me. I don't need a national following. As a sensitive introvert who requires vast amounts of space and quiet, I don't want a Marjorie Holmes level of recognition. And yet. And yet. And yet.

    Chris Woods was the first person who believed in my writing enough to publish what I thought would be my only book. I wrote <u>Life's Too Short for Dull Razors, Cheap Pens, and Worn-Out Underwear</u> to answer a friend's "double dare" to write what I thought about while I ran distance miles. After what I thought was my "Hey, look! I wrote a book. A one-and-done" effort, Chris challenged me to compile my online FROG Blog posts into a book of essays. My inner prodding asked, "There are already eight million book titles available on Amazon alone, why add your word weight to an already-obese book market?" Chris recommended including other people to create an anthology, which evolved into book #2: <u>The FROG Blog: Learning on a Lily Pad</u>. Neither of those books had initially flown off store bookshelves. Eighteen positive online reviews hardly warranted writing a third book. And yet. And yet. And yet.

    A line from Toby Keith's song <u>American Soldier</u> kept playing in my mind. "I don't do it for the money, there's bills that I can't pay. I don't do it for the glory, I just do it anyway."

Gulp! I filled my lungs with a slug of air and, with shaky FROG legs, I jumped into waters that chilled me to the bone with fear.

Tenacity and determination teamed up and boiled over when I was reminded that, with God, I'll live to tell this story. FROG stands for Fully Rely On God. I need to firmly stand on God and write what He has called me to do. <u>KNEE DEEP: A 9-Month Whirlpool of Handwritten Letters to the Creator.</u>

Christina M. Eder

A Writer's Prayer
By Sarah Hamaker

Dear Jesus,

Please guide my writing today. Help me to write for an audience of One, striving to please you first and man second. Give me the right words to bring glory to you.

Keep my heart attuned to the things of heaven, rather than the things of earth. Don't let my desire for earthly success draw my attention away from my Savior. Give me a humble and teachable spirit, never thinking I am above learning or too busy to lend a hand to a fellow writer.

When I find myself discouraged, let me find comfort in your Scriptures. When I find myself wanting more than you've seen fit to give me, let me rest in the knowledge that I am exactly where I need to be on my writing journey.

Help me to not lose heart when the days are dark. Help me to seek after you when my heart hurts from rejection. Let me see glimpses of how my life is furthering your kingdom.

Above all, allow my words to bring the light of Christ to those who read them. May my love for you shine through all that I write, even when I don't even mention your precious name.

May I write for your glory and may you use my writing for my own good.

Amen

Author's Note

I talk to God in a stream of consciousness through these letters. As I've been typing this, my editing hat is crumpling, yet I press through toward authenticity. What will become of this? Absolutely unsure, I nevertheless trust God to guide me, one letter at a time, one word at a time. One leap at a time.

Eyes wide open, taking big gulps of air as I jump into this life lesson from the lily pad,

Christina

(I sometimes use the pseudonym Felicity when I've felt a sense of spiritual conversion. Other times I may even sign off with a heart, a smile or no signature.)

KNEE DEEP:
A 9-Month Whirlpool of Handwritten Letters to the Creator

Jesus,

Thank You for guiding the words that You want on my business card. It doesn't list any degree or expertise. Simply, "Christina M. Eder, Author and Lover of Handwritten Notes."

I want to be remembered for one thing: Christina M. Eder, Encourager. My eulogy can be short: "She lived under an umbrella of sunshine. Now let's get outside, gather under the gazebo and enjoy dark-chocolate treats in her honor." ☺

Thank You for big messages in few words.

Thank You for big messages in few words.

Love,

Christina Daughter of Our Father

Christina M. Eder

Creator,

   Thank You! Today I'm living a version of things I've watched on the Hallmark Channel. I'm energized, relaxed, wanting to cry from pure pleasure to write.

   I treated myself to a short road trip to Sweet Café in Norris. You showed off in the already-quaint setting by adding extra touches to my strawberry, spinach and walnut salad. I sat on the cafe's patio and its window sign reads, "The Lord is Risen." A yellow butterfly greets me before she dances to the hanging purple flowers in a nearby basket. The 10 Commandments, on a permanent old-fashioned chalkboard on the side of the building, affirms today is the day my intentions must align with action.

   My eyes would savor a nap right now, but if Robert Frost were joining me on this picnic bench, he'd say, "But I have miles to go before I sleep."

> **A yellow butterfly greets me before she dances to the hanging purple flowers in a nearby basket.**

KNEE DEEP

With forward motion and accelerating E-motion... I write on. A sugary kiss back at You!

Christina

Christina M. Eder

Counselor,

*   Thank You for hearing my silent cry from the passenger seat of life while You took the wheel. Tonight, even though I'm disappointed and agitated, I discovered that an instant apology and thank You helped me immediately rise above my hurt.*

*   You showed me how to fully love through apologies and gratitude. Thank You for guiding me to swiftly forgive and accept apologies.*

*   Love,*

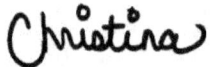

Father,

Thank You for the treasure of our son. I value him more as an adult than I did when he was a child. I appreciate his interaction with his three daughters and wife. He's a natural father, embracing each activity and teachable intersections. I think I would have learned about healthy parenting through his example. He blends struggle with tenacity and patience (for the most part). He celebrates growth.

> I allowed doubts to wreck much of the joy many parents embrace.

I was so afraid of failing as a mom. I often worried the tone of my voice or any misguided lessons would scar him. I didn't want him to adopt my weaknesses. Maybe shying away from motherhood was my pride... I feared making mistakes that would stunt his growth. I allowed doubts to wreck much of the joy many parents embrace.

Lord, I wish I had "given" our son to You completely when he was born. Thank You for my husband. He's been a rock-strong father. Tig had

Christina M. Eder

Dad worries and pains, yet he raised our son with persevering courage.

Help me forgive my Mom regrets. Thank You for allowing me to witness the pure love our son shows in his roles as husband and father. He isn't perfect, but he loves. Despite earthly pangs, he loves from his heart.

Grateful that You are the perfect parent,
Your Daughter

Your Honor,

    I sit in this courtroom, waiting to witness a custody case. The dad wants more time with his little girl. The mother wants more money. The child has become a human basketball tossed into the stands of an opposing team.

    My heart breaks as I watch people's lives change at the tap of a gavel. Jesus, I cry to You for all children. Their basic need for security and love is threatened because of parents who refuse to surrender their greed and selfish docket. They need Your child-protective services!

    Please convict all parents to surrender to Your ruling. Guide every judge to sincerely consider the child as a whole person. Let them not allow vast numbers of family cases to wear them down. Guard them against judging from a weary stand or impulsive short-term verdicts.

    As a witness for You, infuse supreme forgiveness into my heart. Let truth reign so there

> **My heart breaks as I watch people's lives change at the tap of a gavel.**

Christina M. Eder

is order in every court. Help me honor Your constitution the way You established it.

    Court dismissed,

Christina

Jesus,

It may sound like I'm talking out of both sides of my mouth, but I'm overwhelmed by outreach requests. I gain energy from helping others. I thrive when I encourage others, especially the underserved or people starting something different. There are so many charitable organizations and creative individuals. I don't know which ones to support.

> **Please grant me discernment between unwise ventures and foolproof investments.**

Please grant me discernment between unwise ventures and foolproof investments. Guide me to spend time, money, energy and words to promote others, but not at the cost of distraction from Your plan.

Help me recognize I'm not obligated to feed or pet every barking dog on my way to eternity. With Christmas season on the horizon, I understand there is more mail and solicitation. Please give me clarity about which requests are good ideas or God ideas.

As Your daughter, move me forward according to Your "Operation Christian Child,"

Christina

Christina M. Eder

Creator,

How do I discern priorities?

Thank You for blessing me with many interests and an insatiable curiosity. I value living with verve, but sometimes this excitement to capture abundant joy leads to unfocused movement.

I yearn to travel. I want to train to be a hospice chaplain. I'd love to lead a book club. I see myself starting a retreat center. I want more new authors to tutor. I yearn to teach more workshops. I crave long and meaningful conversations with people who seek spiritual depth.

What is action and what is distraction?

So how do I decide what is important? What order You want me to do them? I treasure Your guidance in "Be still and know that I am God." How do I blend quiet discipline with awareness that my earth time is expiring?

What is action and what is distraction? I don't want to waste time overthinking an answer. I need Your prudence to hone which opportunities You want me to respond to... and when.

Thank You in advance for peaceful clarity. I don't feel Your peace right now, but I write this as a trust offering that Your faithful action and timing will follow.

Christina M. Eder

Lord,

    I understand that being a self-employed author and life coach involves advertising, but I find myself distracted with marketing. I'm not a minority in a world that is saying, "Enough is enough!" People are saturated with information. I limit my media posts to weekly frequency, but still feel like I add weight to an overflowing tub of electronic waves. Drowning. Being drowned out. Drowning others with more choices.

    You've given me gifts to write and speak encouragement. Thank You for allowing me to dive into Your plans. Keep me from drowning in distraction that sails me away from my Lighthouse. Help me wisely choose what to publicize. Teach me to write Your message with living water from a purified filter.

    Remind me that I write and speak for You,

Christina

Jesus,

Thank You for caregivers, counselors and mediators. Some of these workers are booked for weeks in advance because so many people are hurting. Heal us from the inside. Give counselors wisdom, clarity, patience and strength. And encourage them to begin and end each session by seeking Your guidance. Minister to both client and counselor.

When these peacemakers get weary or irritable, renew their positive energy. In heaven, we won't need health professionals because we'll be completely healed and whole. For earthly purposes, nourish these unsung warriors.

Lovingly concerned,

Christina M. Eder

God,

Thank You for greeting cards. I browse card departments and find them therapeutic because I can match a sentiment to whatever my heart holds that day.

Thank You for illustrators who design color into these cards. Thank You for humorists who provide comedy relief through their messages.

Thank You for writers who infuse enough humor into their messages to make me laugh out loud, right in the card aisle!

Thank You for artists who create tranquil nature settings or soft light hues to invite calm to the card.

Thank You for authors who craft words that express what I'm trying to say. Thank You for writers who infuse enough humor into their messages to make me laugh out loud, right in the card aisle!

Thank You for courageous writers who bare their souls by penning their pain. In sharing their understanding from hurtful experiences, I adopt a spirit of compassion. I feel less like an island because they expose a wound that often relates to my heartache.

Thank You for greeting card creators who honor less-publicly discussed situations, such as miscarriage, chemo treatments, adoption or couples who are separated.

I appreciate cards that celebrate people born on holidays, or for men who are like a dad, or women who have been a mom/motherly figure. I can't imagine going to a card shop if I were blind or illiterate. Thank You, Lord, for the treasures of eyesight and literacy!

Love,

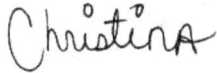

Christina M. Eder

Shepherd,

    Thank You for third-shift superstars who care for Your creation while many of us sleep. Shelf stockers, truck drivers, cashiers and servers in 24/7 businesses. Thank You for overnight maintenance workers, soldiers, security, prison guards, just to name few of these superstars.

    Thank You for servants who work on call: clean-up crews, law enforcement, hospice, medical, cab drivers, parents, funeral-home staff.

> **Thank You for third-shift superstars who care for Your creation while many of us sleep.**

    You see what these evening shepherds do. You know every family sacrifice they make to adjust to job-related alerts. Please grant these families a patient understanding while they are separated when their loved ones answer their duty call.

    Refresh them when they grow weary. Protect workers while they labor with little to no sleep. Guard them against hopelessness when they wonder if anyone cares or notices their contribution.

Thank You for their integrity when they question their stamina. I never thought I'd say it, but thanks for my short experience of working the graveyard shift. That opened my eyes, awakening me to appreciate laborers who work non-standard hours. I'm increasingly grateful for my daytime employment and working conditions.

Thank You for all the workers who fulfill missions You've assigned them to, no matter what shift or circumstances they face.

Faithfully,

Christina M. Eder

God,

My heart broke when I saw a road crew having to scrape a dead animal from the middle of the road. I fight the urge to cry or become grossed out when I see an animal – especially a dog – lying on the road. Today's sighting leads me to ask You to bless these highway workers in a special way.

I understand these road warriors are employed to pick up trash or highway debris. And I can grasp the hassle of heaving broken furniture that has been dumped or fallen from a vehicle.

These crews face the hot summer smells and frigid-temperature discomfort.

These crews face the hot summer smells and frigid-temperature discomfort. Strengthen them as they lift, clean and discard the "less than beautiful" elements of a fallen world.

Thank You for allowing me to see this sad reality. These road workers widen my scope of gratitude and remind me we are created to care for Your earth. Help me remember to be faithfully excellent in whatever road You call me to minister.

    Love,

    Christina

Christina M. Eder

Messenger of Truth,

    Thank You for postal workers and delivery drivers, especially during heavy-volume mail season.

    Thank You for their year-round commitment. They address all weather conditions, customers, animals, traffic, schedules and job-regulation changes.

    I find it ironic that the U.S. Founding Fathers declared – in writing, no less! – "One nation under God," yet new mandates require government services to deliver mail on the Lord's Day. Please guard my heart from growing bitter or weary from watching the world's laws overstep Creation's guidelines.

> **Encourage mail carriers and delivery drivers to carry words of light in their minds and hearts as they deliver packages and envelopes.**

    Encourage mail carriers and delivery drivers to carry words of light in their minds and hearts as they deliver packages and envelopes.

Strengthen their desire to receive Your forever stamp of approval.

    I'm en route to being returned to my Sender,

Christina

Father of History, Father of Eternity,

Thank You for the angel workers who serve memory-care patients. Grant them compassion to repeat tasks that patients forget.

Show caregivers how to love each person mindfully, no matter what state of memory they are in. Soothe any restless spirit that plagues a forgetful mind.

Give caregivers gentle ears to hear — especially when they've listened to a repetitive story. Help them use their patient's story as an audio legacy.

Let our earthly angels know we all need frequent reassurance and displays of endless compassion. When our patience lapses, strengthen us.

> **Soothe any restless spirit that plagues a forgetful mind.**

Thank You, Lord, for a sound mind. Protect me against Alzheimer's, dementia or mental imbalance. If anyone I love faces memory-care burdens, please align them with diligently kind caregivers.

Encourage me to selflessly love when a world forgets about others.

Jesus,

Thank You for a fun and creative way to pray for my family and friends! Today, while I was waiting for a meeting, I opened my phone's contact list. As I went through each name, I pictured each person's face. I visualize them smiling, which helped me be less focused on how long I'd been waiting in the lobby.

When I "see" each contact on my phone list, I thank You for that person. If a friend or family members has a situation that needs prayer, guide me to make their request to You.

Funny that I was just getting into the phone-contact prayer rhythm and I got called in for my meeting.

It's going to be a terrific day! Thank You for this jump start! Gotta scoot!

> **Thank You for a fun and creative way to pray for my family and friends!**

Christina M. Eder

Jesus,

Thank You for reminding me that not every barking dog needs to be pet or fed. I've frequently found myself connected to needy people craving worldly recognition. These starved-for-attention people have consumed much of my energy and time.

You've created me with a genuine yearning to elevate others. We all thrive when we are encouraged. However, somewhere along my mission, I've allowed myself to think I need to encourage or cheer on everyone instead of "only" the ones You've given me.

> **Thank You for reminding me that not every barking dog needs to be pet or fed.**

I'm grateful when someone shows up in my thoughts, prayer time or path, but I need to watch that I don't become distracted. I don't need to send everybody a card, phone call or followup. Sometimes my faithful prayer is "all" You require.

Guide me to focus on Your mission. I am

not riding solo, and I'm not the pilot! I am a passenger on Your plane. Guard me against elevated pride.

Love,

Felicity

Christina M. Eder

Surprise Maker,

You are the originator of surprise parties. You plan adventures into my daily festivities. You invite an extensively varied guest list and serve a buffet of sweet and sour food.

Today has been a day of horn blowing and chaotic party games.

Metaphorically, sometimes guests throw confetti or smash cake onto my walking path (a.k.a., not always a red-carpet treatment).

Today has been a day of horn blowing and chaotic party games. I've had to face the music when several dark tunes played out (i.e., a lot of rhythm and blues. Read between the lines, Lord: heavy on the blues, light on the rhythm).

While I write this evening reflection, thank You for helping me recall the candles from this day. My sister gifted me with a call to tell a hilarious story. Thank You for her contagious laugh.

A hospital patient watched the rain pour outside his window and arranged valet service for after our visit. A high-school girl stood in a group of friends who were on their phones and when I walked by, she made direct eye contact and smiled. Thank You for people who take the initiative to reach beyond their agendas and comfort zones.

As I mentally clean up from today's festivities, tuck me under Your protective covers. Prepare me for tomorrow's celebration of life.

Christina M. Eder

To my Heavenly Music Maker,

Thank You for the radio/CD player Tig bought me. He knows how music is vital in my life and how bummed I got when my old reliable boombox wore out. He understands I don't care for the computerized methods of streaming and downloading music.

Thank You that he went out of his way to hunt for the most basic CD/radio with an old-fashioned wire reception antenna.

Thank You for the gift of hearing and having the luxury of choices.

I'm grateful for music variety. I've found radio programs that teach about parenting, character building and positive approaches toward living with Eternal vision. To some people, this CD/radio gift may seem simple, but I appreciate Tig's respecting my need for simplicity.

Thank You for the gift of hearing and having the luxury of choices. Guide me to listen to music and people that create music for my soul. Tune me in to the frequency of Your airwaves.

Christina

Creator,

   Thank You for a universal need to create. I create with my literary voice. Others create through music, construction, teaching, marketing, pastoring, coaching, cooking, art.

   We want the world to notice us. Even shy, introverted people (like me) hold some level of yearning for others to see us, to listen. We need our uniqueness acknowledged.

   Lord, You crafted all heavens and earth. You invite us to explore Your art gallery. I have not perfectly responded with gratitude. Some of my creative offshoots have killed the purity of Your heart.

   I've watched a creation of chaos birthed from a dire need to be heard. I've witnessed imaginary truth that doesn't regard devastation, that eventually follows temporary deception.

   Whatever I create, please paint Your Light on the canvas of my heart. Prepare me for daily showings of Your bright colors and peaceful hues. Guide me to display a collection of gentle tones, showcased in an exhibit of life-giving creations. May my aspirations complement You, my Creator.

Christina M. Eder

To my Eternal Light,

    You are the creator of natural light. Last week, a friend gave me a light box as a winter solstice gift, so today I write my prayers in front of it.

    This artificial light falls pale compared to Your sunrises, noon-day brightness and sunsets, but it keeps me from hibernating into a black hole of inner doom. Daylight Saving Time and cold weather nearly paralyze me.

Daylight Saving Time and cold weather nearly paralyze me.

    I feel closest to You when I have abundant sunlight and warmth. I'm grateful for light-box designers who invented this bright substitute to bridge a gap between downtrodden and uplifted spirit.

    Shield me from dark thoughts. They only add presence to an absence of light. During these weeks when the earth rotates to share light with other parts of the world, thank You for this artificial supplement.

    Thank You for the generous friend who understands how sensitive I am to seasonal darkness.

Jesus,

You are a prime example of bookends. The Alpha, born in a humble barn. The Omega, dying on a crossbeam of humility and love. Both sources of wood. Each supported a different cause. All finished with a new birth.

> **Teach me to suffer well and understand You wouldn't have created tear ducts unless they were meant to be used.**

You cried Your first cries when You entered this world. You cried Your last cries when You left this world. My tears cry joy. Sometimes I sob from the heart, a cry that leaves my ribs sore.

You promise there will be no tears in heaven (and I hope You have other jobs for our tissue makers)! Until then, remind me it is natural in this life to cry. Teach me to suffer well and understand You wouldn't have created tear ducts unless they were meant to be used.

I'm curious to see the salty-water jar You've collected from my earthly tears. Thank

Christina M. Eder

You for reading all that is shelved between the bookends of my life. Thank You for knowing me, cover to cover!

    Love,

    Felicity

Lord,

Thank You for a lunge of courage. This is hard to write on paper because seeing my heart on paper exposes pride — pride birthed even though my original motive was purely conceived.

I've used the praying-hands emoji on my phone to text people who come to mind. I've reached out more frequently through emails and postings to let others know I'm thinking of them.

You are the One who came to give life. You have saved the world.

BIG You, LITTLE me.

In this world where so many people are lonely, getting lost in the crowd and not heard among the noisy chaos, I've taken it upon <u>myself</u> ('my' being the first indicator of pride) to initiate connection. The more people who have appreciatively responded motivated me to increase my frequency to connect with them.

This morning, I hit a panic button because I hadn't heard from a few people in a couple of weeks. Instead of recognizing that it's Christmas and New Year's, I worried that they would think

I wasn't faithfully praying or didn't care.

I've realized many relationships have grown one-sided because I've trained people that I'll be the one to initiate check-ups, check-ins and outings. Rein me back in, Lord! Guide me back to using one method of outreach and then waiting for their response before using another method to reach out. (i.e., I leave voice mail. No answer? I try emoji text. No response? I send card. I. I. I. ☹).

After writing this, now it seems silly; yet I felt compelled to expose it. You already know and knew it's been there. Thank You for Your reminder that yes, there are hurting, lonely people; but I am NOT the suicide-prevention specialist. You are the One who came to give life.

You have saved the world. BIG You, LITTLE me.

Thank You for initiating this contact. Guard me from wayward actions. I respond with gratefulness!

Your turn, Communicator! ☺

Lord,

    I've forgotten my primary purpose... to write for You! As I've published more books and created an online presence for networking, I've gotten speared by the world's baited traps.

    Instead of writing for several hours in the morning while I've been fresh (like I used to), I've allowed myself to write a piece long enough to publish and then hurry to check email or do a posting. I've allowed the world to dictate my schedule instead of checking with Your original plan for what YOU want me to write each day!

    I'll continue this later. I feel that You're not allowing me to ponder this with a condemning approach. Convicted, not condemned. I'll come back to review this after at least a week of writing and editing. Until then, thank You for this quick grounding!

    Refocused,

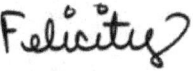

Christina M. Eder

Lord,

    Thank You for the veteran I just met. We were on the greenway and I saw that his legs have been partially amputated. He used wheels while I use legs to move forward.

    He joked that he doesn't usually initiate conversations with people, but for some reason, today he decided to accept our conversational intersection. We were both in a dark spot and talked about needing to get outside for natural light. Thank You, Lord, for today's sunshine.

    You gave this man courage. He exposed his heart, deeply embedded with shrapnel. You know his war experience has caused guilt and grief. Please replace his shame with Your forgiveness.

> **You chose *me* to be the first civilian to whom he confessed his burden!**

    Jesus, I am humbled by this veteran's trust. You chose <u>me</u> to be the first civilian to whom he confessed his burden! Help him know it was safe to open fire on his pain and that I'll faithfully support him in prayer.

    Thank You for showing me that as planet soldiers on earth, we may walk on healthy legs, yet remain spiritually paralyzed. As a wounded warrior on Tour Earth, keep me from falling victim to enemy attacks.

Thank You for putting me in fox holes with soldiers like this war veteran. Instead of merely saying we're one nation under God, align us to become one *universe* under God!

Taking a shot in the dark,

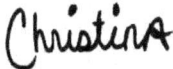

Christina M. Eder

My Army General,

    I'm struggling with decision overload. The abundant choices of this world have expanded beyond my ability to decipher good from great.

I understand every thought isn't meant to be bought, but I've become overwhelmed from sifting through now, later and never decisions.

> **Sometimes I feel like an undisciplined child being turned loose in a mall with a platinum credit card.**

    Sometimes I feel like an undisciplined child being turned loose in a mall with a platinum credit card. (I'd really be in danger if the mall was filled with bookstores!)

    Lord, grant me wisdom to choose the best action without obsessing about how I use every penny, minute, word or invitation.

    Thank You for a sound mind and the luxury of living in a country of plentiful resources. Thank You for listening to my prayer while I filter through the world's clouds and smoke screens.

Encourager,

Thank You for awakening me to untamed anxiety. I've had a growing fear that has no root. Wintertime. More darkness and less heat send me into a penetrating physical freeze. Emotionally I shiver.

I'm in a warm protected environment, yet spiritually shaking with chills. I fear I'm not living up to my potential and feel restless. You have instructed me to be still and silently commune with You, yet I panic that I'll grow complacent or miss Your direction.

Thank You for reminding me that anxiousness isn't a sin. Weakness isn't a fault.

Thank You for reminding me that anxiousness isn't a sin. Weakness isn't a fault. Only when I don't ask for Your help does it become an open door for darkness to blow cold into a gap between me and You.

Retreating from You leads to rebellion, deceit and difficulty. Protect me from the temptation to shrink because I doubt Your love or forgiveness.

I'm physically cold, so please light a fire

Christina M. Eder

in me so I don't become spiritually lukewarm. Insulate me with reassurance that my earthly journey includes weakness, practice and failure. Help me draw close to warm myself by Your fire.

    Warm in Your arms,

    Christina

Deliverer of all mail,

Thank You for the kindness of our postal service! Our granddaughters mailed us a card and used stickers instead of postage stamps on the envelope.

Someone at the post office had simply written "These are not postage stamps. Postage due=.55." They sent the letter on a COD trust that the recipient would cover the stamp charge.

> **They sent the letter on a COD trust that the recipient would cover the stamp charge.**

I don't know who began this path of kindness or how many people graciously followed it, but You continued their generous trail. That bright-blue envelope traveled from Kentucky to Tennessee on a loan.

Opening the mailbox this morning to find a hand-addressed card to Grams and Gramps was already a treasure. This pay-it-forward delivery loan was like receiving an oversized package overnight expressed to my doorstep, a gift of smiles to my heart.

Christina M. Eder

    Please rebound each postal worker's generosity with Your abundance. Thank You for all people who go the extra mile to show kindness every day.

    Love from Your grateful daughter,

Creator,

Thank You for a spring filled with chipmunks! I don't recall a year when I've seen so many of Your curious stripers. They remind me of mini sea otters as I watch their frivolous exploration.

I sat by the pond tonight and watched one hop, looking like he wore a mischievous grin. The little guy looked like he was sneaking up on one of the turtles or geese on the bank.

I see rabbits, birds, butterflies, squirrels and, of course, chipmunks, living in fairly close proximity. Respecting, observing, interacting and playing with each other. Simply doing what they were created to be: a chipmunk, a turtle. A catfish, a crane. No agenda, no competition outside of their circle of survival. No bickering. No verbal communication beyond what is necessary for them to simply be.

Thank You for these creatures infused

Christina M. Eder

with free-spirited character. You've created them for us to learn from and enjoy. Thank You for the gift of eyesight so I can learn through visual observation.

    Love,
    Your Curious Daughter, Christina

11-26-19 (2:50 a.m.)
I'm not able to sleep so instead of counting sheep, I'll go to the Shepherd with these disturbing contemplations.

How has this world turned into an evolution of delusion? When did it become socially tolerated to drop the F bomb, yet people are tortured and killed for talking about God?

> **Who would have thought social media could have produced such anti-social loneliness?**

Who would have thought social media could have produced such anti-social loneliness?

Why does comedy have to involve laughs that inflict pain on another person? How can someone's injury or risk be defined as a "practical" joke?

Historians, Google researchers or psychologists may have statistics or answers, but at a surface level, with a 3 a.m. outlook, I'm sad to wake with such an explosion of depravity.

Help me from growing weary. Thank You for listening to me in the middle of this night. Soothe my soul so I can go back to sleep.

Christina M. Eder

Physician,

    I sprained my ankle and foot. I'm irritated by slow healing because I don't want to arrange my schedule to accommodate foot soaks and ice therapy. I also rely on regular walks to reflect and seek Your guidance throughout the day.

    As I sit here with my leg elevated, I sense You are reminding me to be still. Help me appreciate what I can do. Guide me to surrender this temporary pain as minimal sacrifice compared to the suffering Jesus bore on the Cross.

> **I pray for people who are in constant pain... some because of broken bones, some because of broken hearts.**

    I pray for people who are in constant pain... some because of broken bones, some because of broken hearts. I pray for people in wheelchairs, especially war veterans who've lost limbs. Penetrate them with Your peace.

    Provide for laborers who face long-term disability after a job-related accident. Restore every one of us from the inside out. Help me lift my attention toward what I can do and trust You to carry what I cannot.

This prayer began when I was consumed by pain. I end this "be still" time physically sore, but mentally and emotionally elevated. Thank You for healing on its way!

Christina M. Eder

Source of Clarity,

   I'm toeing a fine line between blending and opposing thoughts. In my effort to understand integrity at a deeper level, I've found myself in a confused state. I've tried to box life into a yes-or-no checklist.

I've tried to box life into a yes-or-no checklist.

   I need Your clarity to focus my mind. There's a gap between the following musings and I need Your blended balance.

Excellence	Excessiveness
Free-Flow	Complacency/Lukewarm
Living on earth	Preparing for heaven
Contemplating	Obsessing
Outreach	Savior complex

   While I'm waiting for Your wisdom, help me wade (not frantically dog paddle ☺) through this whirlpool of thoughts. Thank You for gut checks. Protect me from self-traumatizing through over-analysis. You remind me: Love the Creator. Love His creation.

   Seeking to understand,
   Felicity

KNEE DEEP

To my Source of Clarity,

    Thank You for a mantra to steady my mind: "Not every thought needs to be bought." In this Christmas season, there's no snow but there's a flurry of activity. My mind searches for visibility beyond a blur of decisions.

    Thank You for an abundant amount of people to love and give to! I'm blessed to have dozens of hats to wear. Like an array of Christmas treats, You've given me delicious ways to serve others.

    Keep me from getting snowed under in an effort to gain traction on my walk with You. As I bundle up to face this December morning, remind me to put on my helmet of salvation (I need one with fleece lining for these frigid temps). Cover my feet in peace, a spiritual form of snowshoes.

    Love,

    Christina

> **Like an array of Christmas treats, You've given me delicious ways to serve others.**

Christina M. Eder

Creator of Joy,

You've penetrated a cold rainy winter day with perpetual sunshine! I received three packages in the mail today, which are like early Christmas gifts of gold, frankincense and myrrh.

I smile as I write this and look at such personalized surprises—a candle and dark chocolate; a music CD and frog coin purse; a 10-disc audio set from a favorite author.

I'd call each of these givers immediately, but my immense gratitude may sound like gushing. For now, I write my thanks to You, the giver of all. Please bless these people abundantly. When the emotional surge of gratefulness tones down, guide my words to be wisely gracious in thanksgiving. Help me be generously wise but not overdo or gush my love.

Love,

Christina

> **You've penetrated a cold rainy winter day with perpetual sunshine!**

KNEE DEEP

Jesus,

    Thank You for the Christmas parade last night! Our small town trumpeted a big-band sound of joy. Lights, people dressed as reindeer and elves, music, Santa shouted Merry Christmas. The crowd bundled in layers of blankets, cradling hot-chocolate cups handed out by members of a church group. Our noses dripped from the cold, but our faces poured out smiles.

> ... today, those wrappers look like confetti, reminding me of the celebration.

    This morning, as I walked part of the parade route, I replayed last night's smile when I saw strands of tinsel left over from a float and a tag from Santa's hat. Ordinarily, I'd be upset to see candy wrappers littering the road; but today, those wrappers look like confetti, reminding me of the celebration. An abundant flow of optimism birthed hope as I reflected on this parade of life.

    Love,

Christina M. Eder

Father of Time,

    Thank You for the seasoned teachers who remind me that learning and practice never end.

    I have one gentleman in his 80s who talks about his struggle with pride.

    A new widower, after his 60-plus years of marriage, faces a spiritual journey beyond organized religion and church membership.

    My 92-year-old friend feels she hasn't contributed much to the world on a larger scale. I wish she knew the deep impact she's contributed to <u>our</u> family in the 20 years we've known her.

    Another friend, who after 78 years, gathered the courage to pursue prison ministry, organized an outreach. But now her husband's health has declined and she's homebound, caring for him. She selflessly tends to his needs but confided how "selfish" she feels when she yearns to pursue her own goals outside of the home.

> **Please remind all of us to be teachable and willing to seek Your truth in this classroom called life.**

I had a one-time conversation with a WWII vet who still wars against anxiety and forgiveness of the past.

I'm grateful for these people who have been generous in trusting me with their deep pains. Please remind all of us to be teachable and willing to seek Your truth in this classroom called life.

Love,

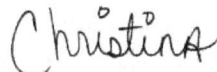

Christina M. Eder

Organic Creator,

Thank You for heightening my awareness of how I use nature in my writing. I use environments to reference human experiences such as "a hurricane of emotion," "a blizzard of mail," "mountains of leaves to rake."

> I honor You when I show up for life as a well-mannered guest.

In reviewing my previous writings, I see frequent references to Your animal kingdom: "acting like a bear," "curious as a pup" or "awkward like a newborn giraffe."

Thank You for scenery to reference. Thank You for changing weather patterns to teach that sunshine and rain are catalysts for growth. I'm grateful for Your natural provisions of light and water. I'm also appreciative of manmade products such as sunglasses and umbrellas ☺.

Help all earthly inhabitants respect the piece of Eden You have created for us to temporarily use. I know this is not my Forever home, so I honor You when I show up for life as a well-mannered guest.

Remind me to clean up after myself; offer

to wash dishes; speak kindly; and use food and supplies in moderation. I respect Your house rules.

    Thank You for providing Creation as a practice field for our future residency in Your Kingdom.

    Love,

    Christina

Decipherer,

    Thank You for helping me choose a word for the year to practice. I've chosen "decipher" to develop my character.

    With two books published, it's been a year of significant learning curves and abundant invitations. In a quest to align my needs to Your wants, the word "decipher" will focus my attention on <u>Your</u> edits and revisions for the story <u>You've</u> written for my life.

> *... it's been a year of significant learning curves and abundant invitations.*

    Help me decipher between good ideas and God ideas. I'm writing these reminders to decipher. They were inspired by a friend's quote, "Every dog isn't meant to be fed on your way to destiny":

    Every thought isn't meant to be bought.

    An introduction could be an invitation or distraction.

    Every person isn't a partner.

    Write for one fan (the One fan of mine created all other fans on earth ☺).

All emails aren't top priority.

Share the market.

Be thankful but not indebted (i.e., not everyone needs to be "liked" on Facebook or receive a review, follow-up call or email check-up).

Decipher. Purify. Sift. Filter all thoughts, ideas, assignments through You.

Thank You, a year in advance, for ways You'll grow me to decipher between Your ways and my ways.

Love,

Your discerning daughter, Christina

Christina M. Eder

Lord of Clarity,

    You have given me newfound sense of purpose with short, clear directions! Thank You! I feel like a FROG in a blender: multiple ingredients mixing a high-speed chase, using the world's recipes.

    I've had intense revelation and equally heightened disturbance. Wholesome food for thought spinning with jaded blades of pulverized (i.e., partial) truth.

    I need Your pulsating power to process this emotional/mental/physical concoction. I'm aware of Your presence and crave a stirring of Your spirit rather than the grinding pace of my own thoughts.

    Thank You for hearing me above the world's commercial-sized mixer noise. This journal entry is like my prayerful recipe card. Help me serve from Your table with ingredients of joy and gratitude.

    Love, Christina

P.S. Hope You like puns and a play on words. Jesus spoke in parable language too. ☺

Jesus,

It makes me sad to hear people talk about Your birthday as enduring a marathon rather than an endearing celebration. Advent should be a time of quiet waiting, but commercialism has materialized this quiet time into a noisy retail tradition.

You came as a baby to bring Light. The world has raised a Christmas spirit that has grown into a darkened sky, filled with manmade stars. **How have original stargazers become today's navel gazers?**

I look at one neighbor's elaborate home and yard décor. I see another neighbor rushing to make children's costumes, bake treats, buy gifts and host parties. They dart in and out of their cars, but what mission are they driving?

Please use my overcast prayer to shine Your Light. Do not allow my eternal Christmas spirit to freeze in a stable. Mature me to generously share Your gifts all 365 days of the year.

Love, Christina

Christina M. Eder

Lord,

　　Thank You for the gift of writing. I had allowed Your gift to hibernate because I grew discouraged after publications weren't buying my material. I never really considered myself competitive until I entered an aspect of a crowded arena of published authors.

　　I'm unsure how to handle this newly discovered competitive nature. I just want to write. The marketing piece has polluted my peaceful motive. While I wait for Your guidance, purify my heart. Infuse Your wisdom into my writing, invitations and assignments. Help me follow Your prompts. Make me content with Your edits.

　　Love,
　　Christina

> **The marketing piece has polluted my peaceful motive.**

Eternal Homemaker,

    Thank You for being my translator. I was trying to talk to a carpenter who is remodeling a long-neglected home in our neighborhood. I've walked past this decrepit house for years and prayed that someone would fix this eyesore. I began seeing a Dumpster outside the house and it was quickly filled with only You can know what. I've watched that eyesore of a house being remodeled, but today was the first day I saw the renovator.

    The man doesn't speak English, but we were able to understand a dual thank you. Our shared smile spoke a universal language.

> **I've walked past this decrepit house for years and prayed that someone would fix this eyesore.**

    He may not have understood my specific compliment, but through a broken "thank you," smile and hand gestures toward the house, I could see we spoke a mutually appreciative language.

    Please protect his hands and bless his spirit. Encourage all of us to construct relational bridges. Tear down walls of neglect. Thank You

Christina M. Eder

for guidance about Your building and maintenance codes.

    Renovating my heart's interior,

Christina

Jesus,

    I just read a statistic from a poll that discovered more than 50 percent of Americans suffer from loneliness. The article discussed the irony of being lonely in such an interconnected world. Are we living <u>inter</u>connected or <u>inner</u> connected?

    Timely statistic, because I've been looking for someone to produce podcasts and video. Many techy people say, "That's easy." Or, "I'll help you"; but when it comes to following through, they are overbooked. How do so many people manage to remain lonely if they're so busy or overscheduled?

    Guard me against judging people's priorities. Keep me from growing jaded when my own wants and needs aren't addressed. Show me how I can be a friend to the lonely. Connect the needy and lonely with people who can (and will!) assist.

    Thank You for inviting me to be a companion to Your people.

    Love,

Christina M. Eder

Jesus,

    Thank You for a message from my study Bible, "Love sometimes demands that we act in very practical and even uncomfortable ways." I'm in the thick of this **PUSH: Pray (and Persevere) Until Something Happens** "love them anyway" scenario. Instead of using this paper and pen to lament, help me write prayers to request a release of selfishness. I want to push forward!

    Love. It's not always practical and sometimes intensely uncomfortable, bordering on volatile! Create a soft landing in my heart to make way for this hard truth. PUSH: Pray (and Persevere) Until Something Happens. Help me PUSH through pain so I can birth new life out of these labors of unconditional love.

    Love,

Jesus,

Thank You for my Daddy! I just got done talking with him on the phone. He has a wicked cold and is facing another Christmas separated from Mom, who is with You in Heaven; yet he remains hopeful and upbeat.

Daddy has his house decorated, lights hung and hosted a family gathering this month. If she had her choice, Mom would have kept a Christmas theme in our house year-round. Now I get to see how Dad keeps her spirit alive. He isn't much for the extra-commercial hype of the holidays, but he loved how lively Mom became when she started playing Christmas music. She'd parade around the house with animation. Her already-generous spirit would multiply around holidays and celebrations.

I think the only thing Daddy buys into during this season is chocolate stars, because it's one of the few times that stores stock his favorite candy ☺. With or without chocolate stars, he follows Your and Mom's display of love without counting costs.

Help me remember Mom's enthusiasm and Dad's generously caring example. Guide my eyes to decorate my home in an uncluttered way but fill it with love.

In Your spirit, all 365 days of the year,

Christina

Lord,

Thank You for the book of Malachi. In reading it, I learned that he's defined as a minor prophet. He wrote a major message! Malachi wrote during the 5th century B.C., when a remnant was rebuilding Jerusalem's temple. They were building during a time of spiritual apathy. These builders promised to rededicate the temple and renew their covenant with God. Instead, they allowed non-believers/uncommitted followers into the temple. No matter how many times they tried to rebuild it, their half-hearted and misguided practices led to the temple's collapse.

> **No matter how many times they tried to rebuild it, their half-hearted and misguided practices led to the temple's collapse.**

I can relate to the builders. In my human effort, I maintain schedules, relationships, projects or activities that are sometimes out of Your framework. I'm sorry for assuming that You'll be perpetually merciful until I decide (eeks... I decide) to check Your building plans. Guide me to

Christina M. Eder

stop my construction and take time to listen and respond to You!

    Love from one of Your weakened builders,

    Christina

Lord!

    Thank You for a fantastic Sunday with Tig! It's been months (possibly years?) since we've experienced such renewal in our marriage. We talked about our prayer journals, read a poem to each other, sat face to face, listening to a "nature's sounds" CD and savored a glass of wine with some dark chocolate.

    We ate dinner at Wendy's and, to some people, this may not sound like a location that deserves such applause. To us, it was a 5-star dining experience because we talked without a time limit, with no agenda. Unlike many of our typical conversations, we didn't have business topics to discuss.

    We listened attentively and mutually asked questions. We laughed. There wasn't that familiar "let's fix this" or "tweak that" tone. Twenty-six and a half years of marriage and yesterday felt like a first date laced with a history of wisdom because we were in tune with each other.

    Thank You for reinstating fresh energy into our marriage!

    Love,

    Your original bride

Christina M. Eder

Jesus,

    I hope there are thunderstorms in heaven. I love the sound of every kind of thunder and rain (as long as I'm protected and sheltered).

    Last night we had an unusual winter thunderstorm. I got out of bed to lie in our guest room, where I could hear it better. The rumble soothed me and, even though the winds were high and shook the windows, I felt a supernatural peace. I'm grateful for our home being strongly built and pray for those who live in less structurally sound houses. I pray for all the homeless who don't have the security or comfort to rest where it's warm, dry or cozy.

    Even as lightning grew sharp, I anticipated the thrill from cracks of thunder that would follow. I typically cringe at noise; but last night, these booms invigorated me. I tried to stay awake so I could appreciate Your entire storm show, but later woke huddled in a blanket, ready to return to bed.

Thank You for Your gift of thunderstorms and providing every secure luxury that allowed me to enjoy Your show.

Love,

Your storm-chasing daughter

Christina M. Eder

Jesus,

    I just got back from walking to the mailbox. It's windy and bitterly cold. As I fussed about layering up, our local homeless shelter came to my mind. Please connect homeless people to employers and mentors who will lead them to jobs. Release the unsheltered folks from addictive chains and bring them out of darkness.

    I pray for all volunteers and workers at homeless shelters. If I'm to reach out (beyond prayer) to donate supplies or hours, please make my heart willing. Today, if You call me to minister in that way, my shivering self says no. I need Your nudge toward loving in action, which sometimes requires discomfort. Grow me to be selfless and actively compassionate.

    Thank You from a daughter practicing for my eternally warm Home

Lord,

    Thank You for creating me to be sensitive. I have often been told to lighten up or stop being overly sensitive. As I've gotten older, I see this sensitivity working to increase my awareness of spiritual discernment.

> **Sometimes what I may think is discernment is really my own misconception.**

Guard me against judging from misguided thoughts. Sometimes what I may think is discernment is really my own misconception. Teach me to blend caution with compulsion, to wisely consider without obsessively pondering.

    Grow me to think clearly, pray purely and walk surely. Thank You for reframing my perception about believing sensitivity is a weakness. With Your guidance, thank You for using this gift for Your glorious purposes.

    Love,

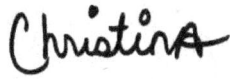

Jesus,

    Thank You for helping me find a podcaster who interviewed an author who said, "A parent is significant but not sovereign." This one sentence produced a double blessing of clarity.

> **... as much as I love our son, You love him more.**

    That reassured me that as much as I love our son, You love him more. That statement releases my control! I'm an important piece of raising a child, but not the only piece that You provide that child.

    Remind me (often) that I'm self-traumatizing when I replace unrealistic greatness with human fragility. Protect me from ego-related pressure.

    Thank You for life-giving podcasts, books and Divinely inspired material to develop my knowledge of Your sovereignty.

    Love to a **Large Creator** from a small me.

Jesus,

    This morning I have optimistic anticipation of what You're doing and how You're moving. Things that didn't make sense have sudden clarity and I find myself joyfully restless.

    A lyric from the song "The God I Know" sings, "the harder I try, the colder I feel." I've listened to this song countless times; but today, that line honed a lesson You've been working on in me.

> **Things that didn't make sense have sudden clarity and I find myself joyfully restless.**

    As I go about this day, I'm tempted to jump up and start organizing and purging material things. Thank You for disciplining me to sit and put pen to paper while You guide and temper me. You can do more with a <u>little</u> of my focused attention than what I can do with <u>a</u> <u>lot</u> of self-imposed assignments.

    Thank You for helping me listen to Your priority list. I'm excited to see what You have tucked up Your robe sleeve for us to do today!

    Love,
        Christina

Christina M. Eder

Lord,

    Thank You for teaching me how fear of forgetfulness could become a pride issue. Worry over absent-mindedness could be a way of saying, "Lord, I don't trust You to help me recall what I need to speak or do as needed."

> **Release me from this controlling distraction.**

    You say You'll equip me with WHATEVER I need in the moment, yet I panic if I don't write it down or do it immediately. Release me from this controlling distraction. Help me practice trust by checking Your memory. Filter what needs to happen according to You.

    Thank You for a nearly immediate pressure release when I wrote that truth. Convince me that Your truth is all I need to remember.

    Love from a daughter You've created with a sound mind

Jesus,

Thank You for showing me how to become a woman of integrity. You chose simple actions to point out how today's choices showed (or didn't show) integrity.

Nearly effortless actions such as returning a movie that wasn't worth renting; paying a bill early; calling a downtrodden friend when I wasn't up for her potential weariness... these develop integrity. You see my actions, so I don't write these examples to try to impress You or draw attention. I write them so when I periodically review these prayers, I'll be reminded to avoid shortcuts.

> **Nudge my immediate obedience, especially when I'm able, but not willing.**

Nudge my immediate obedience, especially when I'm able, but not willing. Thank You for Your valuable teaching.

Love from a student on earth learning about heavenly qualities,

Christina

Christina M. Eder

Jesus,

    Thank You for recurring messages from two different sources that reminded me of Your pace. You walked from town to town. You walked on water. You tell us to walk humbly.

Remind me to slow my thinking and align my steps with You.

    This message confirmed what Norman Vincent Peale wrote about in <u>The Power of Positive Thinking</u>. He noticed how older clocks have longer pendula that result in slower-rhythm sounds than newer clocks with shorter pendula, which swing faster. He said it's almost as if the clock's pace is signaling us to pick up our pace.

    I believe these messages teach me about the pace of electronic communication. Posting, scrolling, screen glare, quick internet access, computer speed — all of these have increased. This fast-moving flow has disrupted my stream of consciousness. I find myself agitated and unnecessarily anxious when I'm on the computer.

    Help me balance my time to recognize that as an author, today's communication methods are necessary. Guard me against losing peace because I'm trying to outdo the pace You want me to walk. Remind me to slow my thinking and align my steps with You. Thank You for checking my motive for motion. Thank You for holding my hand so I'm not trying to run ahead of Your speed.

    Love,

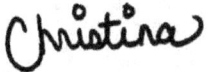

Christina M. Eder

Jesus,

    I got a 2-for-1 special of understanding! You pointed out why I'm irritated about general society living with a worry of the future instead of living with a wonder of the present. I've been putting 72 hours of pressure on my 24-hour fuse. (Now I've become short fused and have overloaded my circuit. ☺)

> **Thank You for installing me with Your spiritual surge protector. Help me frequently use my dimmer switch.**

    Please help me shut off this self-powered switch so I can recharge and receive Your power source. Thank You for installing me with Your spiritual surge protector. Help me frequently use my dimmer switch.

    Love from Your in<u>fuse</u>d daughter

KNEE DEEP

Lord,

    I watched a documentary about the Dalai Lama. The reporter showed his surroundings and monastery. The Dalai Lama's quiet personality is married to joyfulness. He loves people in a simple way, not in crowded celebrations done in his honor. Interestingly, fanfare events that are intended to honor him actually <u>dis-</u>honor his pure flow of quiet gentle joy.

    I've been searching for a hermitage, spiritual retreat center, a remote place to write. As I sit drinking hot lemon water in my home studio and listening to a nature sound of rain CD, I realize I already have what I thought I was looking for. I've unknowingly created my own monastery-like conditions. Thanks to You, I've seen Your gracious provision. You said, "Peace, my peace I leave you." Today, I've found what You left behind for me. Thank You!

> **He loves people in a simple way, not in crowded celebrations done in his honor.**

    Love from Your peacefully evolving daughter,

Christina M. Eder

Jesus,

    My heart yearns for personal connections that don't require a screen or appointment. I miss picking up the phone to call someone to talk. Now people text or email to schedule a conversation or outing.

    People talk about how busy they are. You've created us to be active, but busy seems to be a buzz word. What are people busy with? So much personality is lost through scripted chatter. Communication has become continual and quick, but I wonder how many texts could be avoided if someone just called to speak through confusion, tone and voice inflection.

    I find myself getting heated as I write this plea. Thank You for listening. Remind me (often) to appreciate quality conversations when I <u>do</u> have them. Move me from a saddened state of "why is our culture this way?" to a creative renewal. Guide me to personalize interactions.

> **My heart yearns for personal connections that don't require a screen or appointment.**

Thank You for listening. Your voice is the one I need (and often the one I want first ☺). Thank You for speaking to my heart.

Love,

Christina

Christina M. Eder

Jesus,

Thank You for an in-person visit with my friend Sue! She talked about restoring her lost joy through a piano that needs restoration. After years in storage, the piano requires work, but she said her piano-playing skills also need fine tuning. ☺

> **Whenever I made a mistake, she reminded me to smile and keep playing toward what I knew.**

She recapped her first frustrating practices. She hit many sour notes. Her fingers used to flawlessly glide across the keys to create beautiful music. With perseverance, they will again. She's restarting her piano playing. Thank You that I get to witness her determination. She is trying to keep from getting stuck by comparing her proficiency with her present capability. Thank You for granting her endurance.

I'm also grateful for Your reminder of Joan, my childhood piano teacher. Whenever I made a mistake, she reminded me to smile and keep playing toward what I knew. She encouraged me to visualize mastering the piece flawlessly until I was able to play it without error.

Like music, guide me to continue reading Your word. You create harmony and melody. When I hit a sour note that doesn't match Your composition, remind me to smile, learn and move on. Thank You for Your encore and interlude of musical mentors.

Love during this earthly rehearsal of Your song,

Christina

Christina M. Eder

Lord,

    Today I took a dozen journals to the Dumpster. You know I use journals to organize, confess, question, praise, request and brainstorm. During last week's retreat, I reviewed them and put them away for future use.

    This morning, I had a strong sense to trust Your recall with what I need. You showed me how keeping written records of so much has created pressure instead of pleasure.

    Thank You for our walk to the Dumpster. Initially it felt like I was sacrificing a lifeline. You reassured me You'll manifest materials when it's time for them to be used.

    On my way home, I chose to replace the word sacrifice with giving. <u>Self</u>-sacrifice makes me think of... well, my<u>self</u>. Giving obediently and freely releases me for Your assignments.

    Thank You for revising my story. Thank You for discovering ideas You've written into my plot line (whether I journaled it or not)!

    Love,

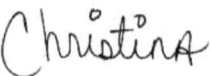

Lord,

    Thank You for the wisdom from older people! They've talked about how they always said they'd take classes and travel when the kids were raised. They'd read and explore when they worked fewer hours and had more money. They've unanimously said that through deaths, loneliness and loss of health, trials remain a consistent part of life.

    Thank You for the 80-something-year-old man who said, "I wouldn't know I was having a rough day unless I had the experience of many smooth days!" Guide me to invite higher learning and elevated thinking no matter what age I reach.

    Love,
    Christina

Christina M. Eder

Lord,

    Sometimes when I jump into Your pool of lessons, the experience feels like an ironing board rather than a diving board. It was especially critical today to give me Your steam iron to press out stained wrinkles from the fabric of my heart.

> You showed me how these assumptions glare with prideful judgment.

    I was drawn to read some of my past writing. I used phrases such as "obviously" or "if I can do this, anyone can." I wrote, "judging by the look on her face," or "I can imagine what he's thinking." You showed me how these assumptions glare with prideful judgment. Even though the words have already been published or spoken, please correct my future tone.

    Thank You for correcting me in front of <u>You</u>, rather than allowing these statements to open a door to future (and perhaps public) humbling.

    Love,
    Christina

Father,

    Thank You for our son calling! We were on the phone when his three-year old daughter needed his attention. Our son also wanted his mom's attention.

    Both of these "children" needed to be heard. When he started getting impatient with her, I reminded him she's never been three years old, so she needed his guidance about when and how to respond when Daddy is on the phone.

    Thank You for reminding me that when Todd was born, I had never been a mom. He had never been a child until we met. We needed to figure out game plays together. Sometimes we practiced like we were opponents instead of family teammates. Thank You for coaching a world filled with rookies on this practice squad for heaven.

    Like Todd when he was a three-year-old, I sometimes arch my back and squirm when You

Christina M. Eder

guide me out of my metaphorical car seat. Guide me to become pliable and allow You to shift and strap Your buckles on me as needed. Instead of pouting or hollering, lead me into gentle surrender with a strong but flexible spirit.

Thank You for this generational lesson between mother, now grandmother, and son, now father.

Love,

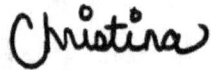

Father,

    Thank You for communication increase with Todd! The more I hear from him, the more I want to hear from him. Together, we've become better listeners. We interrupt less and respect each other more.

    Last night, I got to hear his new plans and instead of telling or directing him as I previously would, I had heightened wonderment. He inspired me when he said, "Right now, I'm lost and need a day to recharge after overthinking."

    Thank You for growing me toward listening-to-understand rather than listening-to-preach.

    Love,

    Christina

Christina M. Eder

Our Father, My Father,

    A quick thank You! Thank You for guiding me to replace "we" with "I" and "us" with "me" when I say the Our Father. This word tweak hit solid when I heard, "give me this day <u>my</u> daily bread and forgive <u>me</u> <u>my</u> trespasses. As <u>I</u> forgive those who trespass against <u>me</u> and lead <u>me</u> not into temptation."

    Guide me to include names of people I need to forgive (i.e. as I forgive "John" who trespassed against me).

    Thank You for this speedy exchange,

Christina

Jesus,

I love how You're having me write these prayer letters to You. It reminds me of how I first talked to You, as a third-grade writer, in my diary.

I've grown accustomed to my writing being edited or published, so I've allowed a cautionary approach to guide my letters to You.

> **Help me discover what You want me to do with this unusual-to-me project.**

Thank You for showing me that when I'm overly concerned about tone, spelling or punctuation, that's a sign of vanity. You called me to write this future book first from unedited depth perception.

I picture this project as being like Anne Frank's diary. She wrote from her heart because she had to, not because she expected that one day her diaries would historically affect a world beyond her own.

Even Mother Teresa felt this earthly yearning for closeness with her Heavenly Creator. [You can read her journal entry, "I Thirst," at the end of this book.]

Christina M. Eder

    Since October 20, I've written these letters and immediately filed them. Until July 16, I'm not to review this nine-month literary birthing assignment. It's January 19 and I'm excited to imagine myself reading our chats. Help me discover what You want me to do with this unusual-to-me project.
    Love,

    Christina

Lord, Father, God, Creator, Rabbi, Wisdom, Counselor, Physician, Jehovah,

You have many names. As a world, we've grown entrenched in splitting hairs about who You are. Thank You for helping me grow to love You as a whole being. You simplify our worldly complexity by making two requests: Love Me. Love My Creation.

> As a world, we've grown entrenched in splitting hairs about who You are.

Thank You for creating one purpose with one truth. We are to be kind to You. Be kind to what You created. Your message is the same. Please unite opinions so we can be made and remodeled in Your one image. Stretch our heart strings to attach with Yours. Strengthen our minds to know You.

Thank You for this facelift that will help me finish my earthly deployment in loving kindness before I meet my Maker face to face.

Love,

Christina

Christina M. Eder

Jesus,

Thank You for Thomas Merton's quote: "If you go out into the desert merely to get away from people you dislike, you will find neither peace nor solitude; you will only isolate yourself with a tribe of devils."

Guide me to see the value of each person without counting cost or calculating an earthly return.

I've had a surge of inner growth due to external circumstances. I struggle with guilt because I feel compelled to physically migrate so I can inwardly move forward. I was called to a solo assignment but chose a partnership agreement, and now I'm carrying a heavy spiritual weight.

Lord, You've seen me come alive in solitude and how I'm at my best when I'm crocheting and praying or writing alone. Thank You for teaching me that I don't need fewer people, I need more of You. Sometimes I <u>do</u> need to turn from people so I can face You more purely.

When I can't see You in people, help me accept that my purpose is to show You through every part of me. Guide me to see the value of each person without counting cost or calculating an earthly return. Thank You for reminding me to use Your armor and face your mission with reassurance of your presence.

 Love,

 Christina

Christina M. Eder

Creator!

Thank you for my new creative writing class! I signed up for what I thought was a one-day workshop and found out it's a 12-week course. Ordinarily, I would have felt burdened by unexpected long-term commitment,

Thank you for reminding me you didn't create me to make money.

but after reading the first pages of Julia Cameron's book, <u>The Artist's Way</u>*, I hope these 12 weeks drag!* ☺

I want to absorb every single part of this renaissance! Cameron writes about "midwifing creative progression." In a magical sense, we're all midwifing Your Creation by birthing ideas and delivering energy. We're laboring to bear what we've been created to do.

Thank you for reminding me you didn't create me to make money. My existence doesn't require a platform to produce gifts You've freely given me. Freely given, free to use. Just as an artist creates <u>for</u> purpose, You create <u>on</u> purpose.

Thank You for this amazing surprise.
Thank you for Julia Cameron's textbook, our moderator, classmates and 7.7 billion other midwives on earth who craft for Your Creation.

Love,

Christina

Christina M. Eder

Jesus!

My closest female friend needs to feel your presence! She has incredible faith, knows you, has watched Your miracles. She's a warrior but she's been spiritually shot down repeatedly. It's January and she lives in a climate that has extended frigid weather and dark conditions.

She's created a fantastic message the world needs to hear.

I've learned so much from her and she's been a rock even while she's faced this four-year frozen desert. She's created a fantastic message the world needs to hear. I don't say this just because she's my friend. You have placed this mission in her.

Kindly and gently shift her verbalized thoughts from, "I must not be ready" to "God's preparing me for..." Prepare her for abundance. Prepare her for renewal. For restoration. For spring air. For summer to bask in Your Son's balmy rays.

Thank you for listening to the details of her story without my needing to write pages of plea and praise. Send (name withheld) sugary kisses from heaven. We believe for your translation and manifestation. Speaking words of life.

I love you!

Christina

Christina M. Eder

Jehovah, Provider,

    I have a financial decision ahead of me. I'm feeling especially generous and want to use my Christmas money to pay off two bills for someone. I've wrestled with this decision for over a month and until I allot that Christmas check, I'm spending too much time examining potential scenarios.

    I joke and downplay money as "dirty green paper" but this week, I haven't been a good steward with my thinking time. Regarding this bill payoff: Is it a good idea or a God idea? Generous or foolish? Is it wise to refrain or an excuse to delay? Show me Your way. Grow my patience to wait for Your clear response. I pray this forward with trust that You will guide me (even if I don't feel it)!

    Love,

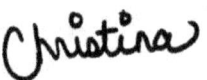

Jesus,

Thank You for a heated home, especially during this January cold blast. You know I'm intensely sensitive to cold, so every time the furnace kicks in, I use its sound to trigger gratitude. I not only have one sweater, one scarf or one pair of socks, but extra ones. (Funny, because after I finished writing that sentence, the furnace kicked off again and it reminded me to pray for people who <u>don't</u> have hot beverages, warm showers, meals, cozy blankets.

I nearly cry when I picture people living in cars or tents. Even though I support homeless missions, I have no idea what they face every day. Continue to show me when and how I'm to use my warmth to generate heat for others.

Gratefully bundled,

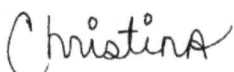

Christina M. Eder

Wise Reflector,

Thank You! In my ponderings about how You've answered prayers, I'm surprised by the ways You've moved.

I asked for media followers. You sent face-to-face friends.

I asked for a technology coach. You sent teammates.

I asked for a slower pace. You allowed my eyes to grow weaker.

I asked for a retreat. You created my mission to work alone with You in silence.

I asked for helpers to lift the load. You provided guides to teach me how to carry the load.

I'd be able to write more examples, but You have other writing assignments for me right now. We'll chat as we go through our day, one word at a time.

Love,

Christina

KNEE DEEP

Lord,

Thank You for listening to my grieving heart. I want to hurry through this painful process. I need Your help to face a loss of familiarity. Grief has been a faithful companion but not a helpful friend. Loss has become a frequent acquaintance.

> **Grief has been a faithful companion but not a helpful friend. Loss has become a frequent acquaintance.**

I don't want to live in this life-sucking habitual heaviness. Give me courage to breathe into this sorrow so I can fully experience it, reconcile it and healthily adjust to move forward.

Thank You for understanding.

Love,

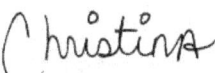

Christina M. Eder

Author of my life story,

    Thank You for a valuable lesson about writing under the influence (of holy spirits ☺). After a flood of revelation, I was so excited to share my spiritual experience with the world that I hurriedly wrote a summary. However, in my efforts to write everything as fast as it came in the spirit, I left out many details and unspoken meaning.

> **... instead of sounding joyful or grateful, I sounded broken with manic energy.**

    I shared this enlightenment with many people but instead of sounding joyful or grateful, I sounded broken with manic energy. A family member brought this to my attention in a kind but pointed way. My stomach sank from the lesson that my spiritual experience might not be understood or interpreted the way You gave it to me. Temper my emotions. Guide my mind to filter Your message. Protect me from over speaking. Thank You for reminding me that not everything You reveal is to be shared with others.

    Guided under Your influence,

Christina

Creative author of my life story,

During my creative writing class, we were asked to define our religion or belief system. This is my answer. What do You think?

> "I'm a spiritual creation on an adventurous quest to explore earth and discover my Creator."

This faith summary makes me realize that, in my efforts to dot is and cross ts, I've allowed my spirit to be weighted. I've focused on 10,000 demand-ments rather than Your simple 10 Commandments. Thankfully, You further downsized Your laws: to love You and love Your Creation.

As a world, we've forgotten how to love You as You intended. We haven't been taught truth about pure love. Sadly, some of us haven't learned how to be loved. We've been tainted by improper displays of love.

Thank You for giving me simple instructions:

Christina M. Eder

Be kind to my Creator.
Be kind to His Creations
Respect my Creator.
Respect His Creations.
Love God. Love His Creation.
Love,

Christina

Lord,

I'm using the deacon's bench my Daddy made me to write this letter to You. He made it over 30 years ago as a housewarming gift for Christmas in our first house. The wood and his craftsmanship have held up perfectly through moves, miles and many uses.

> Just as Daddy's hands guided the creation of this bench, I know Your hands will guide and provide.

It has housed towels, tablecloths, silverware, books, magazines, decorations and dishes. It has been used as an altar.

Just as Daddy's hands guided the creation of this bench, I know Your hands will guide and provide. Help my vision be sharp like Dad's. He meticulously angled and router sawed its pieces. He cut three heart shapes into the frame to remind me his love will outlast his physical life. Keep me from cutting corners.

Thank You for the memory of Daddy in his workshop. I remember the smell of wood while sweeping sawdust, and watching his expressions as he poured joy and sweat into his craft. I wonder what You looked like when You were creating me?

I can't believe how much I recall of Daddy's sayings, quirks and habits that uniquely define him. Thank You for the wood of this deacon's bench and the wood of Your Cross. My earthly father and heavenly Father have gifted me with love that is ingrained, shaped, reinforced and stained with protecting coating. It fills my heart's porous fibers.

Thank You for all carpenters, especially ones like You and my Daddy!

Love,

Your daughter

Jesus,

Thank You for Shel Silverstein, who wrote The Giving Tree. You know this is one of my forever loved books. Today during my quiet time, I grew restless. You showed me how You are like the Giving Tree. I could almost hear Your voice like how I imagine the tree's "voice" in this story: "Come, sit. Play near me. Use my wood. Use my leaves." Like the tree, You give me branches to swing on, apples to eat, a backrest, shade, protection to nest.

> The boy appreciated this giving tree and, as a child, he appreciated its presence. He ran to its familiarity for many reasons. I relate to the older version of this boy. I've used Your resources to build my craft, build my bank account, build my courage... but in my restlessness, I've run off and done my own thing. You have unlimited resources, but I need to restore roots in You before I seek more.

Thank You for giving me two hands so there's one to hold Yours and the other to share what You are giving.

Christina M. Eder

Show me how to walk in the orchard You plant me in. Please take both of my hands as we walk together. Thank You for giving me two hands so there's one to hold Yours and the other to share what You are giving. Guide me to want the Tree more than its produce.

Love from Your daughter seeking solid grounding

Jesus,

Thank You for my trip to Europe several years ago. I remember one of the best things from that trip was freedom from checking email, voice mail and snail mail. My co-travelers carried their connective devices to the U.S. I sighed relief because I told everyone back home that unless there was an immediate-family death while I was gone, I was only to be contacted at the emergency number.

> **I still have that vagabond spirit.**

I've always had the deep yearning to travel. I loved childhood road trips. My dream jobs would have been the Peace Corps, airline attendant, travel agent, cruise-ship worker, teaching missionary. I still have that vagabond spirit. If I am to travel, please align me with assignments and provisions to make this happen.

If this constant yearning to travel is a frivolous whim, quell it. Thank You for the travel I have gotten to do. Thank You for Your protection during my trips. I carry these experiences as some of my fondest memories.

Love from Your frequent flier on memory lane

Christina M. Eder

Lord,

    Thank You for showing me what clothes to clear out of my closet. I don't have many extra clothes because I don't like to shop, but I realize I've kept dark-colored tops, simply because I don't want to shop for brighter ones.

    After this closet cleanout, I have fewer clothes, so I'm encouraged to replace the "practical" navy and black with colors. Guide me to stores, prices, colors and styles that meet the activity needs You have for me.

    Thank You for listening to my simple-to-some-people concerns and joys,

Christina

Jesus,

    I discovered a new way to pray while I was walking. When I'm walking to organize my thoughts, there are houses and decorative touches that catch my eye. I'm not a fan of extra possessions. **I enjoy renting because it frees me from locking into one style of house or location.** When I see something around a house that appeals to me, I've started saying, "Thank You for creative beauty and the eyesight to see it." Today I've added, "If that's something I am to get for my earthly home, please guide me toward it. If not, I'd like that for my heavenly home."

    This pray-it-forward fills me in two ways... to acknowledge appreciation without figuring a way to fill every desire, plus an anticipation of what may be. If something still appeals to me in heaven and it's Your design, You'll have it waiting.

    Please match my desires with Yours!

    Love, Christina

Christina M. Eder

Lord,

　　Wow! I just got to experience a stupendous sunrise that put earthly words to shame!

　　It's a brisk February morning and I wanted to walk longer so I could be enveloped in color. I love feeling the fullness of You when I'm in wide-open spaces.

　　The cold drove me back to my car with a hope and yearning for warmer weather so I can write on picnic benches or a blanket in parks.

　　I head into my Martha and Mary Studio for a new week of writing. I gratefully cherish our spring and summer spots. Thank You for this winter-day sunrise as a prelude to bright, warm sunrays!

　　Love,

Jesus,

Thank You for the nudge to close my eyes to reflect and create gentle distance from the world.

We attended a small church and stood out as visitors. I chose that church because it's small and quaint. I craved to be "unknown" this weekend. Instead, while we waited, many people came to us for introductions and questions. One lady spoke loudly and quickly, and I found myself immediately losing peace.

> **Guide me to keep my heart open and my mouth shut.**

Just as I was graciously going to walk out of church, You encouraged me to stay still and simply close my eyes. This lack of eye contact became a proactive way to distance myself visually. It created a non-abrasive way to gain space between my need for peace and people's want for fellowship.

I pray blessings over this church. Please prosper it, Lord. Guide me to keep my heart open and my mouth shut. When many invitations knock on my door, lead me to know how to

Christina M. Eder

gracefully open the curtains and when to draw the blinds.

Love,

Christina

Gentle Lover of my soul,

    Thank You for Your thought about an ad for a foreign-language course. In addition to learning Spanish, Russian or German, what if kindness was the world's universal language?

    Learning a language outside of our native tongue requires practice. Help all of us to practice what You have taught: kindness, truth, understanding and all love languages in between. That's how You created this world to be. Guide us to speak and live Your kindness. Thank You for seeing goodness in all languages!

    Love,

Christina M. Eder

Great-idea Giver,

Thank You for a new perspective about priorities. My to-do list can become a worldly task master.

Today, instead of "What am I to <u>do</u>?" I'm focusing on "Who am I to <u>be</u>?"

You will always have assignments for me to complete. My to-do list will never be finished, but if I act upon who I am created to <u>be</u>, I can do what You crafted me <u>for</u>.

Strengthen my resolve to become a woman of substance with Your priorities as my goal.

Love,

Christina

> **Today, instead of "What am I to *do*?" I'm focusing on "Who am I to *be*?"**

Lord,

    Thank You for automobile-driven prayers. When I see a car that reminds me of someone who has a vehicle like that, I use that model to guide my prayer. Sometimes I see a car that makes me think of someone I know from a different town or state. Thank You for memories of people that stem from seeing a similar vehicle.

    Please protect us on all highways. Guide me to follow Your one lane of thought. Let my drives become prayer missions.

    Love,

    Christina

Christina M. Eder

Jesus,

Thank You for this morning's mundane house chores before I began my workday. I had a dynamic quiet time with You and my mind is creatively full. Instead of jumping into every exciting venture, You guided me toward mopping, and folding laundry to organize my thoughts. While I did repetitive floor scrubbing and clothes folding, I appreciated the productivity that followed. I was surprised to look back and see a clean house <u>and</u> have a clear head before I even started my work assignments. Thank You!

Lord,

    Thank You for speaking to me through pen and paper. When I write, I sense Your guidance and movement. Thank You for what I now call sandwich-cookie prayers: Thanks. Help. Thanks. "Chocolate" praise, filled with prayer needs, topped with thank You for answers coming. Thank You especially for the times when I have a <u>doubly</u> <u>stuffed</u> "cookie of prayer requests!"

    Keep filling me with Your flavored ingredients!

    Love,

Christina M. Eder

Teacher of Wonder,

When I review my past journals, it's like reading an adventure story. As a curious adult child, I picture myself reading these literary travels in a little red schoolhouse.

I'd like to become a travel writer... stopping at old churches, small cabins, barns, cafés and retreat centers, and writing about each experience. I think it'd be fun to use children's stories to lead workshops and listen to other people's stories.

If this is something You have in store for me, I say yes! When I picture travel writing, I see myself as an excited third grader in front of a teacher who has just asked for a volunteer. I jump up from my desk, raise my hand and urgently wave my arm as if to say, "Ooh, ooh! Call on me, teacher!"

Whatever happens with these writings, I know I'm moving into this day with a peaceful excitement. Check with God. Check my motive. Anticipate Your unexpected.

Love from Your thankful student (being continually filled with lessons and blessin's),

Jesus, Author of my life's plotline,

Writing prayers longhand on blank scrap paper has opened doors of freedom! I have kept lined journals with page ribbons for years. Over the past 10 years, I switched from longhand streams of consciousness to bullet-point praises and prayers. That style allowed me to quickly reference lessons and blessin's; good ideas, random dreams.

> **Now I realize I can verbally talk to You whenever the "pleases" and "thank You"s happen.**

Looking back, I see how I trained my mind to categorize our talks, almost like a checklist. Now I realize I was journaling with an intent to recall every praise or request. I complicated our connection with this tally.

My original motive was to write and trust You with all facets of my life. It became a tedious burden because I feared I'd forget to say thanks or ask You about something. Now I realize I can verbally talk to You whenever the "pleases" and "thank You"s happen.

Thank You for reminding me to allow our

Christina M. Eder

relationship to naturally flow. Keep me from damming up Your pure water stream with my head pollution.

From a heart flowing because of Your well of wisdom,

Christina

KNEE DEEP

Jesus,

You are my Landlord and Homeowner. My peace and trust are the tenant (tenet) of my faith but today I've had anxiety that is burglarizing rooms of my heart. Worry has broken in and is trying to take up residency in my mind.

Thank You for alerting me... peace and anxiety cannot co-exist. One needs to be evicted. **Guard me against allowing worry to unpack its baggage and threaten the trust I've placed in Your Security System.** While I wait and watch You move, doubt and concern lurk outside of the door. Protect me and help me find refuge in knowing You have equipped me with peace and protection.

I wait for serenity to catch up with my words and Your promises... "Fear not. Do not let your heart be troubled."

Becoming courageous as You instruct,

Christina

Christina M. Eder

Creator of my inner monastery,

Thank You for reminding me about what I wished for pre-author and life-coaching business days. When I was in the office scene, I craved to work in a retreat center. I wanted to spend my days at a bed and breakfast making meals, serving guests, writing cards and creating surprise gift baskets for others.

> **Thank You for easing me out of a job situation that made sense to the world.**

You've allowed me to work from a home-based studio. I realize I <u>am</u> living in a retreat center atmosphere, based on the atmosphere I have created. I have monastery conditions where I can walk, write, drink coffee, burn candles and play instrumental music. I enjoy solo lunch periods to read and eat slowly on the patio.

When I have guest-speaking engagements, I enjoy using frugality to create small gift bags for workshop participants. I get to handwrite notes, pray, coach other authors and mentor young writers. Sometimes I get frustrated that my income is not steady, like it was in the business world. Often people label me as a recluse, but I feel the richest and closest to You as my coworker.

Thank You for easing me out of a job situation that made sense to the world. Thank You for the inner monastery You have led me to.

Love,

Christina

Christina M. Eder

Lord,

Thank You for the gift of being able to walk independently. Some of our best talks come from our outside walks. Today, I passed someone pushing a wheelchair to transport a disabled person. I had a gripping sensation, "What if I didn't have use of my legs? What if I needed to rely on someone else to help me walk or to be mobile at <u>all</u>?"

This made me thankful for being able to dress myself, use the restroom on my own, or walk out the door when I want to.

> **Thank You for disabilities that teach me about acceptance, surrender and relying on You and sometimes others.**

I felt suffocated in picturing how different my relationship with You would be if I didn't have privacy, silence or independence to walk out my prayers.

Thank You for this reality check. Never allow me to take my knees, feet, leg muscles or any other part of me for granted. We are all disabled in some way. Keep me from independently running ahead of You. Thank You for caregivers. Thank You for disabilities that teach me about acceptance, surrender and relying on You and sometimes others.

Love,

Christina

Christina M. Eder

Lord,

Yesterday, a participant in my creative writing class was asked to introduce herself. She responded, "Do you want the official version or the authentic version of myself?" She knew what our instructor wanted to hear. The participant prefaced her introduction with asking to speak what was true to her.

Has our culture grown so accustomed to mistrust and smokescreen each other that our conversations have become so guarded?

This dialogue struck me as ironic. Has our culture grown so accustomed to mistrust and smokescreen each other that our conversations have become so guarded? Have we come to expect this somewhat accepted façade?

It's painful to see how people respond to, "I hate x, y, or z" versus "I love God/Jesus." How have we tolerated hate talk about others yet bristle when someone speaks of loving You?

I've observed poisonous rants that pollute conversations. Meanwhile, conversations that talk about loving God stop people dead in their tracks.

Thank You for teachers and influences who have invited and developed my desire to learn about loving You. Guard me from becoming jaded (or stepping on a soap box, ready to bubble over with an authoritative/know-it-all/enlightened tone).

Keep me humble. Fine-tune my ears to listen-for-understanding. I'm not always right. Only You are righteous. Help me pass Your patience and gentle love onto others. I love You, Jesus!

Christina

Christina M. Eder

Knower of All,

 I read a statistic about the human brain and discovered the average intelligent person uses seven percent of their brain. Genius level, according to science, is estimated at 10 to 11 percent usage. I can't wrap my head around this untapped potential You built into us.

I know You created me for abundance, yet I accept meager offerings.

 I simply wonder, if I use seven percent of my brain's capacity on earth, will I get to use the other 93 percent in heaven? I know You created me for abundance, yet I accept meager offerings. Statistically I may use only seven percent of my brain, but I continue to grow my desire to use 100 percent of my heart to love You. Keep joyful blood pumping into the clogged arteries of my soul. That's cardiac arrest prevention. ☺

 Love You with all my heart and know there's room to grow!

Lord,

    You are like my spiritual oncologist, exposing mental cancer. Please use Your radiation to treat the source of what is poisoning my spirit. As I wait here with an IV pen and paper "mask" to receive Your guided treatment, help me follow Your recovery plan.

    As I heal and restore, thank You for creating a clean heart within me. XO

Christina M. Eder

Jesus,

    Thank You for the people who leave me kind voice mail messages. Sometimes in the solitude of a writer's life, I crave connection without needing to go somewhere. I thrive on stillness yet sometimes need to hear a human voice. I save certain voice mails to replay for times of restless loneliness.

    Thank You for sending personal connections when I want an "in-person" voice. Keep me most in tune with Your voice.

    Love,

A Valentine's Letter to God...
Original Valentine,

Thank You for sharing Your love through perpetual Creation. Today I learned listening is a form of love. Simply shutting my mouth and opening my ears becomes a valuable gift. People want to be heard. People need to have someone to love them enough to stop and hear what they have to say.

Jesus, You already know every word I'll say and yet You faithfully listen without interruption. You patiently wait for me to finish crying or gently guide me toward more loving thoughts and responses.

Your gift of love through the Cross would break anyone's bank. Our soul health cost You Your life. Help me to become a lavish giver of listening and loving. Use the health of my mind and soul to love You and others 365 days a year, 24 hours a day, 7 days a week.

Remind me I also need to love myself, so I have a full tank to love others.

Christina M. Eder

With a spiritual box of hearts, stuffed with plush energy and a bottle of Holy Spirits, Love, Your Daughter and Valentine

Lord,

Thank You for hearing a message about Your silence. One of my teachers said when You seem the most distant or quiet to us, that's when You're working the most diligently on our requests. He suggested You are aligning all parts so when it's time to reveal Your answer, we'd be ready, and Your plan's implementation would be smooth.

I love picturing You (possibly wearing wise-looking reading glasses ☺) pondering my life's blueprints. You see who and what needs to be moved where and when. I also need silence and space when I'm working on an intricate project or idea. This teaching reassured me You are working behind what sometimes seems like a "closed door" to me.

Thank You for tuning my ears to hear You in silence.

Christina M. Eder

God,

    Thank You for Your lavish gifts. What if You gave me tomorrow only what I said thank You for today? What if the only way You'd hear my prayers was if I said please?

    I consider myself a fairly polite pray-er. I remember when I learned the Our Father and thought how rude it sounded to hear, "give us this day our daily bread." It sounded greedy. Or "forgive us our trespasses." It still sounds demanding when I say this part of the prayer. I think we should add a few pleases and thank Yous into it.

    <u>Please</u> give me this day my daily bread. Please forgive me my trespasses. <u>Thank You</u> for delivering me from evil.

    In reverent love,

Christina

> What if You gave me tomorrow only what I said thank You for today?

Lord,

    Thank You for a cotton-candy sunrise! I pulled into the Walmart parking lot and watched this jaw-dropping magnificence.

    I wondered how You looked while You created today's colors, clouds and sky patterns. Did You speak it into existence? Do You look at where and how You'll piece our worlds together and simply think it into Creation?

Guide our eyes to look beyond enclosed spaces and discover what You create minute by minute.

    As I walked into the store, I wished everyone could have gathered in the parking lot to watch this glorious sunrise together. I wanted all workers who spend much of their days indoors to get outside and discover what can be found in nature.

    Guide our eyes to look beyond enclosed spaces and discover what You create minute by minute. Thank You for the gift of eyesight!

Christina M. Eder

Lord,

Thank You for the fun idea You gave me to stick surprise notes in Tig's shoes. Today I wrote, "Put your best foot forward" and "Jump into today with your feet firmly planted." When we go for a walk tonight, I'm excited to see his response.

Thank You for simple, unique ways to touch other lives in inexpensive, spontaneous ways. Continue to show me how I can sprinkle confetti of frivolity into each day.

Jesus,

This morning I read from the book of Zechariah. One sentence caught my eye. "The earth was resting quietly." Did "resting quietly" mean peacefully? Was he referring to the quiet rest as people responding lethargically? Were they resting as if unaware? Or resting calmly?

> **I have recently discovered freedom from not needing or knowing an immediate answer.**

There's something resting quietly inside of me as I visualize what that scene may have looked like. I have recently discovered freedom from not needing or knowing an immediate answer. I'm learning to respect other people's responses. This has created restful quietness in my spirit.

Please remind me that when I quietly reach with focused energy, rather than when I strategize to conquer, I receive greater clarity.

Thank You for being my Warrior, Commander of Peace. Continue to guide me toward that restful quietness that Jesus showed. He left peace for us to find and claim. May I search and find it.

Christina M. Eder

Lord,

    I'm glad You gave me the idea to put a daily devotional on my bathroom counter. I've noticed how some of my greatest "attacks" and revelations happen while I'm in the bathroom. When I'm brushing my teeth or washing my hands, now I can read that devotional to nourish my mind. Not only does this practice ward off drifting thought patterns, it provides fresh concepts to consider.

    Simply power-full,

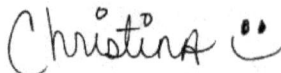

Lord,

    Thank You for using my signature stitch pattern to crochet an afghan for (friend). Others have encouraged me to diversify or try new patterns, but this tried-and-true repetitive action keeps my hands/mind/prayers flowing without being mentally taxing. The methodical rhythm becomes my crochet and pray time.

    (Friend) encouraged me to consider this pattern as my signature stitch. Like a commercialized brand, people will know it's my label when they receive one of my crocheted blankets.

    As I packaged the afghan, I see deeper meaning in the pattern. I use a "3-in-1 V" stitch that connects the strands of yarn. Each stitch is the same, but every blanket is crafted with colors, prayers and thank Yous tailored to the gift recipient.

> **Each stitch is the same, but every blanket is crafted with colors, prayers and thank Yous tailored to the gift recipient.**

    Thank You for (friend)'s encouraging me to stick with my craft. She said how sad she feels

Christina M. Eder

when people try to personalize someone else's signature style on life. Thank You for uniqueness. Within that originality comes spirited creation.

Love from one of Your weavers... a 3-in-1 V stitch. V means Victory!

Maker of Music,

Thank You for my mom's music-box collection of Christmas songs. She and Grandma both treasured music boxes. They have left these for me to enjoy the light tinkling notes.

While I listen to this CD with music-box songs, I picture Mom. She always had a peaceful look when she listened to these. Thank You for the 45 years You gave her to me on earth. I have music of my own to make and anticipate sharing songs with You, her and Grandma when I enter Your musical hall of fame.

Using a (music) box step, my heart that dances with joyful anticipation.

Christina M. Eder

Jesus,

    Thank You for soft sweaters and fuzzy fleece. For many years, I wore tailored business suits. My jobs required crisp, sharp, professional corporate dress. Now with a business-casual style, my clothes reflect Your gentle, comforting presence. My work flows peacefully from soft cloth.

    Love,

    Christina

Thank You for soft sweaters and fuzzy fleece.

Friendship maker,

Thank You for the treasure of a soul mate! She has abundantly enriched me. She tells me that I have benefitted her "more." ☺ We're not in competition but laugh when we joke about how You use our relationship to show Yourself off. ☺

Thank You for intersecting our paths. Our heartstrings don't include four-way stops or traffic jams. It's like a spiritual roundabout in our circle of life.

Please continue to unite us as we practice for eternal life.

Love,

Christina M. Eder

Jesus,

    Thank You for the start of a crocheted blanket. I chose mint and variegated green yarn. I thrill at the energy released from certain colors... this one offers a calming and neutral tone.

Thank You for the start of a crocheted blanket.

    I can't imagine being colorblind. My greatest fear is becoming blind. Whenever I'm preparing a salad, using colored pens, watching nature or looking at book covers, I panic to think how I'd observe the world without color!

    Thank You for the vibrancy You add to my day through Your palette of color. Thank You for Your creative ways to display it! May my colorful excitement never pale or fade!

Lord,

    I'm waiting for my third book to publish and while I wait, I continue writing FROG Blogs and prayers to You.

    I thought I would spend the first year doing book tours, connecting to author circles, have more writing-coach clients and guest-speaking engagements. Instead, You have drawn me into silence, spending much of my time writing notes, thank-you cards, ministering through listening to people in hospital waiting rooms. I know these are Your assignments and Your timing. I ask You to help me surrender and trust Your schedule.

> **Help the world value unity. Guide us to be gentle with each other as we learn Your ways.**

    People ask when my next book is coming out or they expect more to be printed. If they saw the stories and education You're teaching in my soul and spirit, it might look like a loaded medical journal.

    Guard me from pressures about word count or production for public eyes. I wish someone could see through Your eyes and see how You've magnified my focus on Your perspective.

Help the world value unity. Guide us to be gentle with each other as we learn Your ways. You know my story because You wrote it. You see rough drafts, edits, misspellings, incorrect word usage or slanted journalism in my practice for heaven.

Guide me to become a professional job seeker in Your company. Be my lifelong teacher in Your classrooms. You're my #1 seller in large print hardback books... from cover to cover!

Love,

C

Creator of wonder,

Thank You for the sweet story about a little girl who guessed that the seven wonders of the world are seeing, smelling, touching, hearing, tasting, being loved, and her group of friends.

I have not seen any of the seven wonders of the world that are classified as wonders, but like this little girl, I live more than seven wonders of Your world every day. Thank You for seeing words and smelling coffee. Thank You for fleece and soft flannel to touch. Thank You for hearing music. Thank You for tasting strawberries. Thank You for many people who love me. **Thank You for loving me even more than my best friends do!**

I'm grateful for this little girl's story. She's updated my perception of seven wonders of the world and doesn't even know it. Help me value all You have created!

With amazement from Your child who sometimes wonders,

Christina M. Eder

Jesus, Conductor of Music,

    Thank You for the gift of music. Sometimes one song line becomes my grounding mantra. This morning, I heard, "There's no dollar sign on your peace of mind." Last week I heard, "Lay down what's good and go for best."

    Thank You for inspiring people to write positive messages into a sometimes negative world.

Provider,

Thank You for the gift of imagination. Much of what You teach me comes from visuals that connect separate pieces into one lesson. Thank You for Your generous flow of creativity. You give me abundant ideas and sometimes it's difficult to know which ones to put into action and which ones need to wait. Some ideas are simply to create joy, discovery, hope and energy for that time.

Protect my thoughts, ideas or creativity from becoming stagnant, but also guard me against allowing my imagination to run rampant. Focus my attention to use Your gift of correction so I may be Your strong vessel. For myself, for others and most of all for You, my Imaginative Creator!

Christina M. Eder

Lord,

    Thank You for the radio caller requesting a song for her husband who had moved to heaven five years ago. She told the DJ about the special song they shared. The DJ was so gentle

... it's her memories and characteristics that will never run out.

and kind. What really stood out to me was how the host asked, "Tell me something uniquely special about your husband that will help my soul recognize his soul when I join him in heaven." Wow.

    I think about when my mom moved to heaven. She left me some money. Some of it has been used. Some of it has been invested, but it's her memories and characteristics that will never run out. Her spirit cannot be affected by such things as the stock market. She left behind heart treasures through her crafts, traditions, cooking, baking, musical talent, generous outreach, sewing, housekeeping values and a sense of frugality.

    I could go on, but for now Lord, I sign off with thanks for the value of one. One hug. One question. One call. One conversation. One person, one day, one prayer answered. You see it all. Thank You for watching over me.

Please tell my mom and my other loved ones in heaven I love them and how excited I am to get to hug them again.

Heart and soul,

Christina

Christina M. Eder

Courage Keeper,

I just learned there are 365 verses in scripture that say to be courageous, to fear not. That's one for every day of the year. Thank You for Your continual reminder to claim peace — 365 of those times are in writing!

That repetition must be like teaching a child to brush their teeth every day. You remind me to whiten my smile. I've noticed how peaceful people tend to smile often. Thank You for Your daily brushing of reassurance. Rinse me from fear, doubt and chaos. Guard my heart from going down the drain.

From Your fresh-breath daughter...

Lord,

Thank You for Tig's asking me to dance midway through dinner. We usually don't have the radio on during mealtimes, but I hadn't shut it off before we sat down. Since the volume was low, I let it play as we ate.

This spontaneous dance invitation is unusual for Tig, especially when there's a grilled meal in front of him! ☺ He also doesn't like to dance but when this song came on, it reminded him of one of our memories so he surprised me by asking, "Do you want to dance?"

At first, I said no, but after the next bite, I put down my fork and said yes... a surprise to both of us! Help me use this joy to practice spontaneity more often. Guard me from becoming rigid or stiff necked.

Thank You for the gift of surprise!

Christina M. Eder

Lord,

"Thank God!" How refreshing to hear someone exclaim those two words! Two syllables can become such a powerful prayer.

I've seen such public timidity when anyone mentions Your name, Jesus. Thank God. Grateful acknowledgment. Two little words. One big meaning. It invigorated my spirit to hear You get proclaimed credit. I hear people say, "That was lucky," "What a happy coincidence" or "It just seemed to all work out." Encourage me to return their observation with a simple, "Thank God!" Protect me from shrinking behind a shadow of a world view. Guide me to shine Your view (without a trumpet blare or preachy glare).

"Thank God!"

Two little words. One big meaning.

Lord,

Thank You for an unexplainable sense of anticipation for this day. Lately, You've taken me on a journey that has been intense. I don't recall when I've ever been on such an eager, growing, painful development stage.

My joy is elevated. My pain is deep, yet I'm learning how to adjust. You're teaching me to be more purely generous "just because." Encourage me to be continually willing to share a generous spirit with the world.

With this surge of lavish positive energy, guard me from unwisely drowning others with contact. Protect me from signing up for too many activities. Thank You for hearing my prayer and knowing my motive, my meaning.

Seeking generous wisdom,

Christina M. Eder

Perfect Artist,

Thank You for the artists You have connected me with!

I've been introduced to writers, painters, bakers, carvers, candle makers, seamstresses, knitters and cartoonists. They have crafts and need outlets. I'm burdened because I want to help these talented people display their gifts. They say they need sales and acknowledgment for affirmation and fulfillment.

Some of them have become disheartened by little or no market, so they've stopped knocking on doors of opportunity. They want homes for their art. Encourage them to faithfully practice their craft and honor their soul art for You, no matter what results.

I especially want to encourage young artists to do what You've called them to <u>be</u>.

You created us to love and serve You. In Your eyes, life isn't about making a name, title, money or enterprise. I especially want to encourage young artists to do what You've called them to <u>be</u>. Blend Your black and white guidance with colorful shades of creativity.

Please show me how to support these artists. I don't want to mislead them with false hope, but I do ask You to open creative windows of opportunity. Let Your light in and shine brightly!

Christina M. Eder

Lord,

    Thank You for an optical illumination! There is a rock formation that looks like a set of praying hands with fingers pointing upward. Sometimes I get frustrated by my declining vision. My eyes and mind connect differently than they used to. This morning, during my walk-and-talk time with You, I'm grateful for seeing this rock formation. Like a sign of Your reassurance formed in stone.

    Love,

Author of Creativity,

Thank You for an 83-year-old lady in my creative writing class who shared this piece of wisdom today: "Creating anything involves focus with flexibility." The class was talking about fears, waiting for a better time, more money or a project less frivolous before they'd start their creative venture. This 83-year-old lady has focused direction and free spirit.

Help me allow wide berths of flexibility within Your direction. Thank You!

Christina M. Eder

Lord,

    Thank You for reminding me to claim and live the peace You offer. Belief leads to relief. Knowledge is head, wisdom is action. When I'm unwise or restless, guide me to go to You quickly to ask for whatever I need. Thank You in advance for answering my questions and developing wisdom.

    Claiming peace,

Lord,

    Thank You for (name withheld). She taught me how she uses rubber bands as a reminder to stretch but not snap. She pictures wrapping a rubber band around love but not to wrap it so tightly that it crushes. She notices how a looser tension is less likely to make her feel a pressure to control or feel like she's being controlled.

    Protect (name). She has experienced serious health setbacks. Help her snap back. May she wrap herself snug around You and trust the tension You provide. Allow her to be stretched but don't let her snap.

    Thank You for her inspirational analogy using a simple rubber band. I love and care for her deeply. Remind me that You love and care for her even more!

    Trusting Your tension,

Christina

Christina M. Eder

Lord,

    Thank You for the idea to drizzle blueberry juice from frozen berries onto my salad. As I made lunch, I realized I didn't have any dressing and You guided my eyes to the thawing blueberries in the fridge. There was just enough juice to use as dressing. As I sit at lunch today, I smile at this sweet surprise.

    Love,

Lord,

   Thank You for a new approach to address trust and faith. I don't understand all facets of gravity, yet I have faith to accept it. I don't need to understand all body parts to appreciate their function. I wasn't on earth when You created the stars and moon, but I see Your results.

   I'm not a science or math teacher, but I value those who have tutored me in these foreign-to-me concepts. I believe we will continue making discoveries and inventions <u>because</u> of You. You allow each generation to explore something new-to-us. Even though You know everything, You patiently watch us practice living on earth. You created universes and galaxies, yet You invite and allow us to be part of Your world.

   Help me trust You, especially when I can't see or logically prove You. Guard me against doubt when I don't understand. You created logic. You created trust. Help me have faith in my Creator — especially in the unknown and sometimes unexplainable elements.

> **You created universes and galaxies, yet You invite and allow us to be part of Your world.**

Christina M. Eder

Greatest Contemplative,

    Thank You for creating me with great inquisitiveness. I see how C.S. Lewis' contemplative quest sometimes left him in pain when he didn't resolve questions, no matter how many layers he searched. I'm in that place. I want to know You, to believe in You more strongly. I don't care how You came to be, but I long to know who You are. Real. Elusive.

> **Thank You for showing me that while You are still, You are moving.**

    You are like a still-life painting. You remain the same whether You are displayed in a nursery, morgue or museum. That "still life" moves depending on the viewer, light and key variables. People have differing opinions and beliefs about You as the Artist. They question Your art, yet You continue to display Creation. Like a gallery painting, You remain unabashed, unashamed, unchanging. You aren't flattered by someone's insincere appreciation. You don't falter when someone critiques Your art.

    Thank You for showing me that while You are still, You are moving. I'm still moving. I ask for Your leadership to discover levels of Your art galleries!

    Love,

    Christina

Christina M. Eder

Matchmaker of needs and wants,

Thank You for the gift of hearing. Sometimes I need music, a podcast, a phone call, a laugh. Sometimes I need silence and meditation to organize my mind.

> **You teach Your message, sometimes through spiritual sign language.**

In both sound and silence, You meet my needs. You make Your voice heard. You teach Your message, sometimes through spiritual sign language.

Thank You for adjusting my volume according to Your wisdom!

Love,

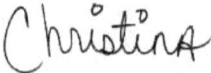

Jesus,

Thank You for an energizing memory! Before (granddaughter) visited, I had blown out my aromatherapy candles. When she walked into our house she said, "Grams, your house smells like church!" I asked her what part of her church experience reminded her of our home's smell. She said, "I don't know which churches they were or where they are, but I remember their smell."

Her association between church and our home brings a sweet scent to my spirit. Thank You for this brief, powerful recollection!

Christina M. Eder

Alpha and Omega,

Thank You for the idea to partner with historical societies to teach workshops. These often under-celebrated groups keep history alive and often struggle with financial backing.

You nudged me to speak at one-room schoolhouses, settlements and small refurbished churches. These events can serve as a fundraiser for them and a place for me to speak Your word in a homey setting.

Thank You for matching my appreciation for small groups in small venues that need support.

Thank You for matching my appreciation for small groups in small venues that need support.

Leader, President, CEO, Manager,

Thank You for a reminder to pray for our leaders. This prayer isn't on my natural radar. I read about how leadership prayers need to be first governed by You, secondly to manage ourselves and thirdly to lead others.

I visualize a flow chart with me in the middle. It starts with You and the rest of us align according to Your chain of command. We need to go to You first for peacefully guided instruction. Each person can be a leader. You've called us to be witnesses.

Help me manage Your company tasks by passing a loving example to everyone. Consider me a good hire, a valuable investment, a wise steward of peace for Your kingdom. Thank You for including me in Your business plan and flow chart for life!

Christina M. Eder

Giver of Compassion,

    Thank You for a compassionate heart. You've grown me to become softer and kinder. My faith is strengthening, and in our alone time, You've granted me encouragement. However, when I go into public or read news headlines, I find myself weighted with sad heaviness. I forget Your calm reassurance.

The elderly, lonely, introverts and sometimes homeless use our library as their community. They need the kind, patient and friendly staff who smile, listen, find resources, or address them by name.

    Today I drove to the library and because of a disease breakout, they are closed until further notice. That library is an office alternative and tremendous resource. My heart hurts because this small library is a source of social contact for some people. The elderly, lonely, introverts and sometimes homeless use our library as their community. They need the kind, patient and friendly staff who smile, listen, find resources, or address them by name.

Please care for our faithful library staff and misplaced community during this shutdown. Help them know their work and lives matter. Protect the lost people who live much of their life in isolation. Guard us from weariness. Help us draw near to You when we are distanced from each other.

Thank You for the comfort of Your warm insulation,

Christina M. Eder

Jesus,

Thank You for instructing me to knock and Your door will be opened. Sometimes I fear what lies behind those doors. Sometimes I want the door to open before You're ready to answer it. Remind me to knock, not pound. Keep me from allowing my internal alarm system to falsely activate because I'm scared about what may lie behind certain doors.

> **Sometimes I want the door to open before You're ready to answer it.**

Keep my hands tightly connected to You—one hand to hold Your hand, one hand to hold Your heart. Seek and I will find. Protect me from eye strain when I'm tempted to squint into the future or focus on making a door open *now*.

Thank You for reminding me to ask (not shout ☺). Ask, seek, knock. These instructions end with, "and it will..." Keep me in Your will, help me trust Your will, help me say I will and <u>be</u> wiling when You answer my call, knock or search.

Gentle Marketer,

Thank You for a fun approach to hand out my business card. You gave me the idea to carry a business card in my pocket and write messages on the card as I give a person a compliment or encouraging message.

I've written such things as, "Thank you for sharing your smile!" "Thank you for your generous spirit" or "Thank you for sharing your contagious energy."

This is a refreshing way to breathe life into someone's day, plus it gives me a "non-threatening" marketing tool that I hope doesn't appear canned. Because of Your out-of-the-box inspiration, I'm excited to find people who share smiles and positivity.

Christina M. Eder

Colorful Creator,

    Thank You for refocusing my attention when I was highly distracted. I am brimming with creativity and want to do everything today. You guided me to write a haiku related to color. That gave me a blend of creative writing and a focus to craft a 5-7-5 syllable work.

    This is my haiku. How do You like it?

Black dots. White Space. What
Color is your palette? Paint
Circles around squares.

    Thank You that I can use color and writing as a form of creative praise to You. You created words, a sound mind and free spirit to craft color into me. Writing is a form of worship when I give it to You.

    Thank You for a bright perspective. Help me color Your world with light. Allow me to see the beauty in all shades of Your creation.

Lord of Fortitude,

Thank You for helping me understand lukewarm living in a unique way. Hot water feels like trust. Cold water feels like doubt. Hot trust mixed with cold (or no) action leads to lukewarm living. Consistent temperance is essential for faithful following.

Keep me flowing with Your hot water. Guard me from allowing cold doubt to drain my trust in You.

Filling up with Your fresh water of understanding,

Christina M. Eder

Great Teacher,

   Thank You for a new lease on life. Fear and trust cannot be roommates. Don't allow my fear and trust to date each other, much less be engaged to one another.

   Marry my trust with Your peace so I can birth creative witness for You.

   Together we never die. We are soul mates. You are faithful even when I am Your wayward bride. I am dying to self so I can spend eternity with You! In earthly death, we will never part!

   Love,

   Your daughter, bride and student for life

Marry my trust with Your peace so I can birth creative witness for You.

Creator of Word Art,

Thank You for a fresh way to look at the word "artifacts."

ART-I-FACTS: blend creativity (art) and facts (science) with You ("I") in the middle.

With You in the middle, I create artifacts through history and legacy. Past and future join present to discover Your Presence.

Thank You for shaping a new expression from a historical word. A collection of artifacts

Christina M. Eder

Crucified Jesus, Resurrected Savior,

Thank You for Holy Week to reflect on Your physical death and spiritual life. You wore a crown of thorns on earth. You finished with a crown of glory for eternity.

Thank You for showing me that in three days, the world witnessed death, waiting and resurrection. Guide me to know that in "only" three days, You changed history. Through Jesus' life, You teach me about death, birth and waiting. All is good and necessary. You get the last word.

Give me courage to suffer well. To wait with a steadfast spirit. To celebrate new life when it comes according to Your promise.

Father of All,

    Thank You for my sister! I got to talk to her on the phone and hung up feeling complete <u>and</u> incomplete — sensing her spiritual closeness but craving her physical nearness. United yet galaxies away.

    When I hear people brag about their sisters, I say, "Wait 'til you meet <u>my</u> sister! You have no idea how much my sis is the best friend in the universe!"

    She is seven years younger and I've learned so much and been inspired through her! In my spirit, I feel that if I tried to explain my fierce, deep love for her, it would gush and sound shallow. Human words can't capture the enormous value I have in Cathy. Other than You, Jesus, she is my MVP on earth.

> **She encourages my ideas with questions. She suggests without trying to solve. She networks and cheerleads for me.**

    She listens, laughs, challenges and holds me accountable without being overbearing. She takes an interest in my entire life and follows up on what she knows gets my heart moving and blood pumping.

    She encourages my ideas with questions. She suggests without trying to solve. She networks and cheerleads for me. There's so much more I could write, but I'm unusually overwhelmed by the depth of this emotion. I want to tell her this in person, but I suspect we'd both be overwhelmed... I'd be gasping for powerful words to describe her impact. And she'd be gasping from overload of my words.

    Please use Your spirit to penetrate her heart so she knows just how sincerely I treasure and respect her for life!

    Love,

Christina

KNEE DEEP

Creator of Literacy,

Thank You for my abundant exposure to outstanding authors! Sometimes when I get overwhelmed by the tremendous writing I want to read, You give me a sneak at what heaven may be like. I picture sitting with every author to hear their story in their voice. I want to hear the story behind their writing. I want their advice about what they learned from practiced process. This eternal visual keeps me grounded in knowing that if it's important to me on earth, I can ask to receive or continue this in heaven.

> **Encourage writers to craft positive hopeful messages to our world.**

Thank You for all teachers who taught me to read. Quality written pieces help me appreciate heaven on earth. Guide me toward what You want me to discover through reading and writing. Encourage writers to craft positive hopeful messages to our world.

Love from Your author on earth. Until I open the next chapter in Your book of life, I write on.

Felicity

Christina M. Eder

Game Changer,

Thank You for a fun thought about how my life sometimes resembles a Ms. Pac-Man game. I picture myself, like Ms. Pac-Man, gobbling up all those little dots along my boardwalk. Colorful ghosts pursue my demise. I keep moving and as they get closer to me, I head toward one of the four power packs that make the ghosts flee.

Spiritually, Your fruit is inner nourishment for my game board of life.

I imagine those dots representing my tiny pursuits because ultimately You have larger power-pack spots in all corners of my game board. The enemies are present, sometimes close and sometimes far, but they're present. They flee immediately when I reach Your power pack.

On the surface, these ghosts are colorful and friendly looking, but under Your power-pack light, their darkly colored motive is revealed. Once they show their base color, Ms. Pac-Man can chase them away. Like enemies, these Pac-Man ghosts are masked in different colors. All pursue her with a destructive intent.

In the world game of Ms. Pac-Man, I have achieved high scores and board game levels. Each level gets faster and more challenging than the previous one. Like Your fruit of the spirit, each Pac-Man board has a different fruit. The player gains additional points when they gobble the fruit. Spiritually, Your fruit is inner nourishment for my game board of life.

Thank You for taking a video game to offer a visual instruction manual.

Love from Your child,

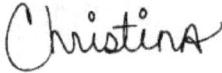

Christina M. Eder

Uniter of All,

   Thank You for comforting me after I read the advisory alert on a public park sign during this morning's walk. With this worldwide health attack, there have been warnings and signs that I couldn't have imagined.

   Wear a mask. Practice social distancing. Practice is required because social distancing is not what You consider natural for humans. You created Eve because You said man was not meant to be alone.

I hear people <u>say</u> they want to be away from people, but in observing how attendance has declined in virtual meetings and events, I think this proves that we desire real connection (despite what we <u>say</u>).

> ... social distancing is not what You consider natural for humans.

   Social distancing is counterintuitive to what You have designed. You tell us to be united as one. I can imagine Your heart breaking when You see Your creation labeled with warning signs. To me, these park signs remind me of Adam and Eve being kicked out of the Garden of Eden. Or what Jesus faced in the Garden of Gethsemane.

A gateway to death, but in the end, You create a passageway to Your eternal garden of life!

Thank You for reminding me to come to You when I'm weary and heavy burdened. Renew our land. Make us healthy and unified. Thank You for hearing my heart pang and loving me through it!

Christina M. Eder

Jesus,

    Thank You for Your answer when I asked You to order my steps. I wonder about who, what, how and how frequently to encourage others. You have guided me in these ways:

I need head pats, play dates and positive words, too.

- ♥ Not every good idea is a God idea.
- ♥ Not every barking dog is meant to be fed.
- ♥ Not every dog wants to be pet (often because it's fearful).
- ♥ Observe body language. Before approaching a person or situation, discern through You first.
- ♥ Include myself in receiving. I need head pats, play dates and positive words, too. Accept others' food, encouragement and invitations.

    Thank You for reminding me that covenant living is a two-way street. In a dog-eat-dog world, guard me against thinking I'm the only foster mom to nurture and adopt all starving animals. Guide me to know my "house space" limits.

    More than puppy love,

Christina

Jesus,

Thank You for a wide-lens perspective! Prior to last week's layoffs, I hadn't heard the term "essential workers." You are perpetually my essential worker, yet some haters consider You non-essential (until they need You for their purpose). I wonder whether haters consider You a threat to their essential quest for power, title, money, possessions and worldly accolades and egos? When I struggle with disrespect, insult, dismissal and all other earthly woes, remind me You call me to be one of Your essential workers.

> **When I struggle with disrespect, insult, dismissal and all other earthly woes, remind me that You call me to be one of Your essential workers.**

Teach us that we are all invited to be workers for Your kingdom. Remove misguided priorities, unwise use of money, time, motive and resources. Spread Your work in contagious doses and encourage us to become Your essential workers. You don't <u>need</u> any of us, but You <u>want</u> all of us. You are vital for healthy living!

Christina M. Eder

    Thank You for taking time to help me see these cutbacks through spiritual eyes.
    Love and faithfully clocking in for Your 24/7 business,

Felicity

Shepherd,

    Thank You for Your consistent message and style. You tell me to take the first step and You are ready to go the distance, eagerly meeting me as I go.

    Draw near to me, then I'll draw near to You. Like Abraham to Ur or Moses to the Promised Land, You said, "Go to the place I will tell you." The lepers were healed as they went (not before).

"Ask and you shall receive. Seek and you will find. Knock and it shall be opened to you."

Help me be faithful in doing my part.

    One message. Two-way communication. Help me be faithful in doing my part. You have perpetually proven Yourself to every generation. Guide me to draw near to You. To go, ask, seek and knock. Help me respect Your timeline and promptly answer Your call.

    Seeking to love You deeper,

Christina M. Eder

Teacher,

Thank You for a modern-day visualization of Jesus coming back to earth. In this entertainment culture I'd be fascinated to see responses if a "Special Feature" message flashed across a screen. I imagine marketing teams advertising a date when people in <u>all</u> theatres and public events would be invited to tune in for a one-time live showing. It would be free and offer a 100 percent guarantee to change everything in their life.

Who would disregard this last chance of a lifetime? Would non-believers change their minds?

All attendees would be offered a refund if the feature broadcast didn't determine their destiny. ☺

I picture You, Jesus, making Your live appearance. How many would attend "The Second Showing?" Who would disregard this last chance of a lifetime? Would non-believers change their minds?

You tell us to keep holy the Sabbath Day. I think it would be neat if You choose a Sunday to make Your showing. It'd be a test to see who is honoring this Commandment.

While I try to wrap my head around this concept, I need to set down my pen and paper to walk and talk with You. Thank You for inviting me to Your heaven-on-earth show.

Love,

Felicity

Your daughter from out of this world as I seek to fully understand You!

Christina M. Eder

Lord,

    Thank You for the statistic about drug use! This seems ironic to write, but today I learned because of stricter shipping regulations, drug dealers have had large access routes cut off. As a result, heroin and cocaine prices have skyrocketed, resulting in less usage. YES!

    Please continue to expose and disrupt these evil business routes! Release everyone from addictions. Help addicts recover. May they trust You to purchase only what You supply.

    With this exposure and surge of arrests, convict us to see Your truth. Give us spiritual eyes. Thank You for giving our world a makeover. Lift our faces to You!

    Love,

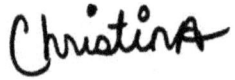

KNEE DEEP

Creator,

Thank You for the breathtaking nature You flood our universe with!

I've had a deep yearning, a need to travel ever since I was a child. That longing has shown up in my desire to major in journalism and become a travel writer. I've wanted to be a flight attendant, a travel agent, a server on a cruise ship and a missionary.

> **Quell my restlessness that wants a travel allowance.**

Thank You for guiding me toward travel videos. This is a light appetizer for my hunger to taste each country's food.

I'm not sure what heaven looks like but I hope I get to see <u>every</u> part of Your universe!

In a strange way, this heavenly visual gives me hopeful anticipation of exploring nooks and crannies without human discomfort, travel expenses, worldly delays or other expected-on-earth woes.

Thank You for this energizing reflection. Thank You for providing my living costs. Quell my restlessness that wants a travel allowance. If You have plans that include writing, teaching

Christina M. Eder

and life-coaching voyages, count me in to Your budget!

    Love from Your vagabond at heart, ☺

Jesus,

Thank You for the reminder of May Day baskets. I remember Mom taking us kids to hang goodie baskets on nursing-home residents' doors. We'd put flowers, candy and crafts that Mom made in those baskets.

> **This has been a fun treasure hunt and I'm excited to mail these surprise envelopes.**

This year, I've used April to prepare literary May Day "baskets." I'm using colored envelopes and stickers and have collected magazine articles, photos, inspirational story clips, and funny sayings. I'll match each collection to a person it reminds me of. This has been a fun treasure hunt and I'm excited to mail these surprise envelopes.

Thank You for simple, creative ways to personalize and give non-traditional gifts via snail mail. Please bless the recipients with joy and love for Your Creation.

Love from Your May Day daughter,

Christina M. Eder

Fitness Coach,

    Thank You for my neighbor who exercises by using activities that children traditionally play. She's middle aged and stays in shape by hopping on a pogo stick in the parking lot. When she works out with her fitness coach, she laughs a lot and the two of them swap frivolous spirit.

> She's middle aged and stays in shape by hopping on a pogo stick in the parking lot.

    Today I watched this neighbor friend ride her bright turquoise "old-fashioned" bicycle. She has a wicker basket and bell mounted on the handlebars. She smiles much of the time in a way that appears that she finds pleasure in celebrating her body's playful moves.

    Thank You for Your gift of my eyesight. I enjoy watching this free soul and have thanked her for her free-spirited example.

Eternal Health Provider,

Thank You for exposing light to a dim world. Through isolation, You have brought people out of their slumber to awaken generosity.

Thank You for all the ways You are healing and rehabilitating our world.

I've got to write a few examples of hope that have been shared in recent news:

One man left $10,000 to each of the four Checkers' restaurant workers who pulled a double shift to cover for coworkers who called out sick.

A woman left a server her $1,200 stimulus check as a tip.

A high-school class is recording a joke or laughable moment. They have set up a hotline and encourage people, especially senior citizens and lonely people, to call for a joke or funny message every day.

People have become more aware of cleanliness and sanitation.

New York City has experienced a drop of 54 percent in smog pollution. People are seeing the skyline through less foggy lenses.

There has been less traffic, decreased roadway litter and reduced accidents.

Access routes to drug deals have been shut down. (Lord, that's one shutdown I appreciate!)

Thank You for all the ways You are healing and rehabilitating our world. Don't allow any spiritual muscle to atrophy after this "exercise in adaptability." Remind us to maintain bulky eternal muscle. We need strength, relief and perpetual healing to walk to heaven, a world without germs and disease.

Healthily in You,

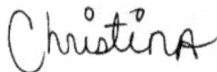

Universal Worker,

    Thank You for the quick smile from a group of Hispanic labor contractors. We speak different languages. We're originally from different countries but today our blood and smiles united to speak a universal language. As these workers laid carpet, they appeared oblivious to the job's less-than-appealing conditions. They knew they had a job to do and showed up with free-spirit energy. They sang native music, laughed with each other, talked lightheartedly, worked hard and then relaxed during their water and lunch breaks.

    Thank You for this gift of faithful workers! Banish racism and judgment. It clouds the color of what everyone can offer when we give them our sunshine!

    Love,

> **Banish racism and judgment. It clouds the color of what everyone can offer when we give them our sunshine!**

Christina M. Eder

Lord,

    Thank You for provision. Today, I find myself wanting trips, outings and material things. Some people have told me I limit myself to a poverty mindset, but I really don't enjoy tangible stuff. I prefer experiences and lavish conversation. However, today, as the weather switches to cooler temps, I need some clothes and money is tight.

    You know I'm needy (in more ways than clothes). Show me Your difference between being needy and being "wanty." You want to abundantly bless me and know I celebrate Your blessings of peace, clarity, steadfast sure footing.

    Thank You for keeping me grounded and rooted in You!

    Love,

    Christina

> **I prefer experiences and lavish conversation.**

Father,

   Thank You for a fresh reality check! I make it a point thank You first before I make requests about needs and wants. Today I started talking to You about needs for friends and situations and thought about how our conversations will be much different in heaven.

   I won't be asking You for anything related to safety, healing, sadness, restlessness or earth-related pain. All that will be left to pray in heaven is thank You!

   Thank You for this powerful pack in few words!

Christina

> **Teach me to generously give and graciously receive.**

Christina M. Eder

Lord,

 Thank You for showing me how I share a trait with Abraham in Genesis 23. His wife Sarah had just died and her burial plot in Hebron became Abraham's piece of promised territory. Ephron verifies this gift is for Abraham, but Abraham doesn't consider himself worthy to accept the land.

 I see myself in Abraham's response. When someone gifts me with *anything*, I immediately feel indebted. I either deny their offer or quickly look for a way to compensate them. A friend taught me that God assigns and uses people to distribute some of his blessings and when I don't gratefully and purely receive their freewill gift, I'm blocking their assignment. She told me I may be denying the giver a test. Eeks when she put it that way!

 Lord, guard me from false pride or misguided humility. Teach me to generously give and graciously receive. Thank You for using Abraham from the Old Testament to teach me a New Testament lesson.

 Gratefully, humbly, purifying,

Grandfather of Time and Legacy of Love,

Thank You for placing two grandpas in my path this morning. They shared how they miss going to church, hugging their grandchildren, talking with friends, neighborhood walks. They miss going to the grocery store or doing errands as a reason to get up and shower. They like to have someplace to go with a mission or purpose.

Thank You for placing two grandpas in my path this morning.

These older gentlemen are part of a growing population, barring no age limit. In these few months of social distancing, there's a not-so-isolated disconnect. Many of us yearn for the previous freedom public contact provided.

Guard us from a downtrodden and timid spirit. Help this be a short-term situation, May our world's facelift include generous hospitality, kind outreach and an eagerness to unite. Protect us from viral isolation. Clear the air so we can leave a loving aroma wherever we go.

Christina M. Eder

Originator of Happiness,

Thank You for a quick way You showed me how to speak sunshine in one word over this chilly morning. While I walked through Walmart, whenever I was asked 'the standard greeting,' ("how are you doing?"), I answered, "Tremendous!" or "Excited!"

One lady stopped to ask me if I was <u>really</u> doing tremendous or just saying that. I lowered my voice in a conspiring sort of way and replied, "Really? I'm not necessarily tremendous right now, but by speaking powerful words, my heart eventually catches up to what I hear myself saying."

It was a fun and honest way to lead, teach and remind myself to speak light.

Love and verbal sunshine,

C

Listener and Audio Provider,

> "I think even my dog will be relieved when I go back to the office. He's used to napping and I'm waking him up to walk him about 37 times a day just to get outside!"

Thank You for the gift of hearing. The worldly impact from this quarantine has birthed conversations that I never expected to hear. Today I feel compelled to write some of the things I've heard in passing:

"I'll be glad when 'all this' is over. I'm tired of it and just want to go back to normal." (Lord, we've gotten used to what 'all this' means and are no longer using words like pandemic or COVID-19.)

"I can't wait to go out for a sit-down steak dinner."

"I'll be so glad when the kids get back into school."

"I'm surprised you recognize me since I haven't had my hair cut or colored for three months!"

"I miss visiting my folks a couple of times a week."

Christina M. Eder

"I need pants and can't even get into a dressing room to try some on."

"I think even my dog will be relieved when I go back to the office. He's used to napping and I'm waking him up to walk him about 37 times a day just to get outside!"

"You should try potty training a toddler when the public restrooms are closed. We were playing at the park and he had to go. What kind of mom am I when I break all appropriate sanitary bathroom training by saying, "Honey, let's just walk behind that tree for now. We have hand sanitizer in the car since there's no sink to wash your hands."

Thank You for this blend of hard-to-believe but animated dialogue. Protect me from weariness. Prompt me to elevate hope and encouragement. Guard me from a deflated spirit.

And in the midst of 'all this,' I have an unexpected anticipation to see what You'll write into our world's story. I know You'll win and am excited to watch Your victory!

Encamped in Your army,

Lord,

   Thank You for listening to my "I wonder when" and "I wonder if" musings. After I talked to You about this health attack, it made me think of what our world had been before the world-wide scare. While we recover from this epidemic, I wonder:

> **Remind us we are passing through on this earthly deployment — a mission to complete before heaven.**

"What new businesses will be created?"

"Which businesses will be closed because they are no longer necessary?"

"How has crime been affected?"

"Will we go back to a 24/7 way of life?"

"What will classrooms look like?"

"What movies and programs will be birthed?"

"How important will sports be?"

"What trends are there in marriages, divorces, engagements, births and family dynamics?"

"Are cosmetic surgeries still as popular?"

"What messages will come out in songs and writings?"

I can imagine there are already studies and statistics about some of these things. Today, I lay these wonderings at Your feet. Have Your way with Your world. Remind us we are passing through on this earthly deployment – a mission to complete before heaven.

No matter what, help us to be kind and gentle with everyone.

Love, Your Curious Wonderer,

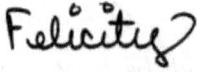

Head of my Eternal Home,

    Thank You for showing me the importance of praying for my husband. Pastor Morris preached about a man's role as a covering over his wife and family. The family is individually responsible for listening and responding to You, but the man's responsibility is to cover his family through Your guidance.

> **Thank You for showing me the importance of praying for my husband.**

    I now see how vital it is that a man needs to first follow You and take Your lead so he can lead. Help men become Your leaders. Urge families to respect and trust their earthly shepherd to guide their flock. Help Tig persevere, discern, obey, grow in strength and patience. Temper his spirit. Align world truth with Your truth, to continually seek Your approval and trust Your judgment.

    Thank You for our progress in learning about roles as husband and wife. Thank You for Your patience while we progress!

    Love,

Christina M. Eder

Lover of Souls,

Thank You for teaching me what love means to You. Strengthen me to love the way You do (minus the crucifixion, please!) Help me be open to Your limitless water—a fountain of love, a fountain of youth. Innocently pure and wisely filtered.

Make me a waterfall to wash others in fresh spirit. I love You the best I know how to today. I surrender the dry parts of myself and ask You to saturate me with Your loving greatness.

Love,

Felicity

Generous Giver of "Little" Abundances,
   Thank You! I just have to write all the small surprises You've showered me with this week! I know I'm missing some, but I must write my thanks while it's fresh in my mind. Maybe one day I'll look back on this to recall such faithful delights.

> I just have to write all the small surprises You've showered me with this week!

- A friend gifted me with a canvas print of baby Jesus, Mary and a lamb. It inspired me to rearrange the layout of my prayer room.
- A cotton-ball massage over my face and neck.
- A neighbor left two freshly picked roses from his garden on my windshield and back window.
- A friend left a goodie bag at my doorstep. Buttercream-frosting scented candle, dark chocolate bar and shower gel with a "Beautiful Day" scent.
- The library allowed me to extend my loan for the "Mama Mia" soundtrack.
- There are more audio options coming out.

> These recordings fill the gap in my visual weakness.
>
> My sister and I had an incredible phone date. We began our talk with two laugh-out-loud stories. We finished with deep, rich heart-to-heart sharing about how she is practicing her word of the year: "accept."
> Thank You abundantly!
> Love from Your little one with big thanks!

Gracious reviewer of my story,

Thank You for reading my heart. Sometimes when I publish something, I wonder who will read it and how they will receive it. Remind me (often) that my most important question is if You were writing a minute-by-minute review of what is coming from my heart, how would You critique it?

Guide me to focus on permanent Godly impressions rather than temporary human critics. You are consistent and true. I, as Your daughter, waver in my opinions (and everything else at one point or another)!

Impress every writing onto my heart and always publish what You want from this loving author,

Christina

Christina M. Eder

Jesus,

    Thank You for the idea to hang magnets with inspirational sayings on our outside door. An elderly neighbor has an alert magnet for emergency workers. When I visited her, that magnet reminded me I have magnets with positive messages on our fridge. I took some of them from the fridge and put them on our front door.

> ... these uplifting quotes serve as a positive reminder to enter our home with optimism and hope.

    Even though we don't entertain guests often, these uplifting quotes serve as a positive reminder to enter our home with optimism and hope. I can invite an attitude of peace and joy each time anyone approaches the door.

    Thank You for this message relocation. From fridge to front door. Location, location, location! ☺

    Love,

Lord,

    Thank You for organizing my day. I had a restless morning of schedule changes and was re-grounding myself when I thought of a quick acronym as a soldier in Your army. I want to be a faithful troop. I ask that You keep me from becoming AWOL in the traditional sense. Refine me to be AWOL <u>for</u> <u>You</u> as:

    Aware
    Willing
    Obedient
    Let You (a.k.a., "Let go, let God")

    Thank You for this sharp, pointed "sword" to remind me I am Your servant today, and every day.

    Love from the front lines,

    C

Christina M. Eder

Lord,

Thank You for the enjoyment and ability to handwrite in cursive. In these days of texting and programmed fonts, I still prefer a hand's art form.

> **In these days of texting and programmed fonts, I still prefer a hand's art form.**

When I toured a museum, I frequently heard people comment on the 1700-1800s exhibits that included handwritten correspondence. They talked about how every letter was written longhand and done in a unique flair. The museum guests were also drawn to love letters. Because of the author's handwriting, those penned words of love seem to retain value.

In my own writing, I notice slight changes in my style, depending on my mood, topic or the time of day when I write. It's convenient to type but when I see my words handwritten, it brings creative personalization. My scripted letters are like a version of a paintbrush on an artist's canvas.

Love from Your creative author of light,

Christina

Universe Creator and Sustainer,

    Thank You for understanding my limited observations. You see the universal picture. From my vantage point, I want to write in the direct light of what I observe on this Mother's Day during this COVID-19 experience:

> **I have written much and thank You for helping me see how You may be using isolation as a building block toward unity.**

People have saved money on daycare by staying home. However, daycare workers have lost income. I see how important it is to have one parent at home to keep up with children and house chores. It also invites the family to see what it takes to maintain a home.

    Prom, graduation and wedding-season alterations have caused businesses to adjust their budget and business techniques. Ceremonial frill isn't necessary for me to celebrate achievements or love. Milestones are measured through people.

    Awareness of social distance. Heightened alert to surroundings and people. There had been a growing trend toward personal detachment, but when it's become mandatory, it seems there's a longing to be closer to others.

Theatre, sports, music and movies have been significantly hit. Without this entertainment, it has invited us to see how we use our time, where we spend our money. We're learning what is valuable and what is surface-level pleasure. I'm also seeing what is, simply, a waste.

More people are walking, biking and increasing outdoor activity in open areas. You give us sunlight, fresh air and bodies to use. We are choosing natural resources over manmade substitutes.

Workers have set up home offices and some are considering their employers' proposals to take pay cuts so they can keep their jobs. So far, statistics indicate at least one third of employees are in immediate agreement.

Gas prices have gone down, air quality has improved. Road rage and traffic have both decreased. You remind me to embrace Your quiet voice and be at peace.

House projects are being tackled and closets are getting decluttered. People are taking inventory of what needs to be done with the space You've lent. I realize how much material wealth we have. You remind me not to put our treasure into things that will rot, burn or be destroyed.

I have written much and thank You for helping me see how You may be using isolation as a building block toward unity. May this pandemic cause us to permanently spread Your truth, priorities, love and virtues. Spirit speaks through airborne waves. Help me spread Your word through my actions. If I need to use words, guide me to which ones You want me to speak.

Love from my observation tower. I look up to You!

Christina M. Eder

Creative Originator,

　　Thank You for an upswing in people's creativity. People are rediscovering their art and crafts. Some are learning hands-on creative ventures. I have seen fun, beautiful, inventive pieces crafted from isolated places.

　　There's also a shift toward minimalism and simplifying. Please blend colorful sprit and generosity over all of us. Give us the means to support and value creative ventures. Thank You for Your example of originality, continually crafting freshness.

Give us the means to support and value creative ventures.

　　You are One Creator who creates all. All for One, One for all.

　　With love in all forms of creation,

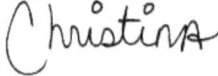
Christina

Wholesome Living Teacher,

Thank You for drawing my attention to the word "prepare."

"Be prepared" has frequently entered my consciousness lately. My interpretation of being prepared is to take what You say and adjust it according to Your intent. Be prepared, in my spirit, feels like I'm readying myself according to You. To accept and follow Your preparation instructions.

When I'm tempted to prepare on my own accord, remind me to say, "Jesus, *You* prepare me so I can *be* prepared."

Thank You for taking THE leap before I take a step. Your big footprints, my little steps.

Preparing to obediently follow in Your footsteps,

Christina M. Eder

Great Listener, Eternal Speaker,

    Thank You for the podcast that taught me that we learn to read through our ears first. The speaker discussed a trend toward audiobooks because people are tired of looking at screens or experiencing eye strain.

    I find it fascinating that we <u>begin</u> reading through voice and then when someone passes away, one of the <u>last</u> body functions to leave is hearing. Even when someone is in a coma or suffers from memory disease, medical professionals encourage people to continue talking to the patient.

> **Through Your gift of hearing, I've learned about listening and understanding.**

    Through Your gift of hearing, I've learned about listening and understanding. Wisdom is developed through two listening ears (before one speaking mouth)! Help me listen with Your ears and use words only when my silent actions can't speak alone. Thank You for everyone who has spoken (and will speak) life and wisdom into our world.

    Guide me to lean into Your voice,

Christina

Warrior, Peacemaker,

Thank You. This morning I'm in my closet that I converted to a prayer room, enveloped in Your quiet protection. I'm eager to get out and explore Your day. I'm reminded of Anne Frank who wrote her diaries in seclusion during wartime. We find ourselves in the middle of a health-scare war and I'm taking precautions to remain healthy.

> **Selfishly, I'm enjoying fewer crowds, less noise, more stillness.**

I'm part of a minority who is getting out of seclusion. Selfishly, I'm enjoying fewer crowds, less noise, more stillness.

If and/or when businesses do reopen, will there be a surge of people suddenly coming out of their "war closets?" I want us to return to health, but also want everyone experiencing this lengthy seclusion to invite a gentler, more manageable pace. There's peace that has come from this extended hush over the world.

Remind us You will use this health "hiccup" for healing in some way. Protect our world's physical health and restore its spiritual

Christina M. Eder

health. Thank You for Your healthy hands and perpetual protection.

    Love,

    Christina

Vibrant Creator of all colors,

    Thank You for our son's sharing his perception about why grey is his favorite color. He liked blue and green as a child, favored black as a teenager and early adult. Now he prefers grey because he associates overcast days with rest. He appreciates storms and rainy conditions that give him permission to rest and lie low.

His job depends on weather conditions and he factored that into his reasoning for appreciating grey. I applaud him for recognizing this.

    Thank You that he patiently listened to me when I explained why purple is <u>my</u> favorite color.

    Thank You for the gift to see all shades of Your colorful world. Thank You for the colorful personalities in all of us!

    Love,

C

Christina M. Eder

Jesus,

Thank You for the surprise thought about the boy in the Bible whose lunch fed 10,000+ people. I picture that little boy being about seven to 10 years old, with a slight frame. I imagine him being approached by Andrew, a rugged fisherman asking him for his lunch bag.

How did he approach the boy? What did Andrew say? Was he asking everyone for their lunch offering, or did he somehow know this boy was the only one who packed a lunch that day?

What went through this hungry growing boy's mind? What convinced him to give up his fish and bread? Did he see his lunch contribution as a sacrifice or as sharing? What impresses me is that this boy did one act that didn't credit his name, yet he gave. He surrendered and his selfless action fed others.

Thank You for this imaginative interaction between boy and fisherman. I can entertain this

> **Guide everyone to generously share what You have already given and promise to give.**

picture in question without pressure to have an answer. I have come to a place where I am more willing to accept questions that may not have answers. I may not need (or want) to know the answer. You choose to answer according to Your timing. Some questions need exploring but with this biblical lunch story, I'm content to simply imagine the scene.

Magnify all sizes of my gifts to feed souls and spirits as You "give me this day my daily bread." Guide everyone to generously share what You have already given and promise to give.

Thank You for this food for thought!

Love,

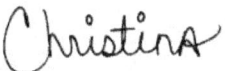

Christina M. Eder

Teacher,

    Thank You for a sermon that taught me how Jesus used the book of Deuteronomy during His temptation in the desert. Today, some people think Old Testament readings are out-of-date or irrelevant. During all three of Satan's temptations, Jesus said, "It is written." His references are all from the Old Testament.

    Thank You for this "well-seasoned" pastor who transformed an "old" teaching into a new understanding. Thank You to all older teachers who share their wisdom. May I always pass along truth in love from what You've allowed me to experience... during times of hard lessons and rich blessin's.

    Keep my heart soft, my mind sharp, my hearing to be in season and to absorb wisdom from teaching.

    Love,

Author of history, future, all eternity,
  You are timeless. Thank You for being here <u>and</u> there. Businesses are starting to open after months of health-related isolation. It's like watching animals come out of hibernation, a new birth, a new marriage.

> **Please guide us to use this rebirth to keep moving from history to eternity.**

Even though there have been innumerable animals, babies and wedded couples brought into this world, for *that* animal, for *that* baby or for *those* two people, for *that* time they are practicing a new life. It blends shock, wonder, excitement, awkwardness, and experimentation.

  New-to-us resources teach about parenting, marriage and living. These are earthly guidelines, not necessarily God lines. Only You are the perfect path and solution.

  Please guide us to use this rebirth to keep moving from history to eternity. Create in us a gentle compassion. Guard us from blaming or expecting one group or leader to "fix" this world's ever-changing moods and wants.

Christina M. Eder

    You promised that every knee will bow when this world comes to an end. Open our hearts, stir our spirit and understanding that You are the only real solution, birthed in truth and eternally loving.

    Humbly and healthily,

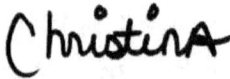

Jesus,

Today Tig and I celebrate 27 years of marriage. We chose each other, in willing love, like You chose each of us. We vowed to love whether we are rich, poor, sick, healthy, better or worse. You're with me through all these earthly vows. You said You'd never leave me or forsake me.

> **Thank You for keeping us grounded and growing in faithful trust.**

Tig and I took vows until earthly death do us part, but You have made Your promise and vowed to be my All into eternity. Sometimes Tig and I have seen rich_er_, poor_er_, best and wors_t_. You have watched us practice living in love, even though many times we may have wanted to bail.

Thank You for keeping us grounded and growing in faithful trust. You know exactly what we agreed to, even though we had no clue what unconditional love and steadfast commitment really meant on May 22 in the '90s. You have allowed tests. Some we've passed. Others? Well, we've individually failed and fallen together. We said "'til death do us part" and we live for the

Christina M. Eder

One who didn't allow His brutal death to stymie His love for His children.

    Thank You that Tig believes in You <u>and</u> follows You. Thank You that I've gotten to watch him increase his surrender, courage and trust in Your family leadership. When it's time for Tig and me to part in earthly death, let the other one be peacefully reassured that You say "I do" forever.

    Eternally in loving awe of You,

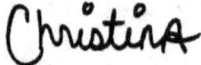

Lord,

    Thank You for our patio. Now that it's spring, I can sit on this wicker chair to read, write and reflect. Tig has been using our patio for his long weekend quiet times. I bought him a reclining gravity-defying chair to relieve his back pain. He bought me two wicker chairs, one for my studio and one for the patio. We bought these gifts at separate times. We bought these chairs while we were apart. We united out of respect for what the other one needed in a chair: reflection and comfortable seating.

    Thank You for this musing. Strengthen Tig and me as we sit at Your feet. You sit on Your royal throne. We sit on our humble patio chairs.

    Resting comfortably with You,

Christina M. Eder

Jesus,

    Thank You for guiding me to write to You while I wait for the carpet-cleaner company. Thank You for on-call workers. Fortunately, I haven't needed to call emergency or on-call workers often, but have enormous appreciation for these faithful laborers.

    While I write through this restless waiting period, thank You for reminding me this carpet cleaning is a first-world situation. You remind me I am to cast all cares upon You and it's okay to go to You for everything, including listless waiting for carpet cleaners. ☺

    Thank You for people who do these on-call jobs, every day, especially those workers with families. Thank You for people who work graveyard shifts or in inclement weather and dangerous conditions to tend to the others' needs. Thank You for the luxury to pay someone to clean our carpets.

    Deeply shampooing from the inside out,

Christina

Provider,

    Thank You for a new way to prioritize and practice my word of the year: "decipher."

    At the end of the day, You invited me to consider: Did I generate more money, or did I generate more kindness? Simple. Powerful.

    Kindly capitalizing on Your Holy Spirit's generosity,

Christina M. Eder

Teacher of few words with much meaning,
    Thank You for guiding me toward an easy-to-remember prayer. This morning You gave me: "May I have an open mind, soft heart, willing spirit and eager obedience."
    Please quicken my awareness so I can learn Your will immediately. Make me a teachable child who embraces <u>Your</u> direction!
    Love,
    Felicity

You've given me abundant insights in a gentle way.

Lake Walker,

    Thank You for bringing me to the lake this morning. I sense that today I'll write short blips to You throughout my day. You've given me abundant insights in a gentle way. While they're fresh in my mind, I need to write these snippets before I leave the lake:

Shepherd,

    Let my mind remain strong and my words be soft.

    Help me be aware without becoming critical.

    Sharpen my vision but don't allow me to scrutinize (or scruten-"eyes"? ☺).

    Grow me strong in wisdom and guard me against judging the unwise or misguided (including myself!).

    Thank You for a TED talk. The speaker said the quickest way to practice kindness is to remember more than six billion people are practicing life in one big world with more than six billion ways to do so. Thank You for teaching me with temperance, at a pace in which I can absorb it.

    I love the ways You part waters and calm seas as I grow in understanding,

    C

Christina M. Eder

Lighthouse Keeper,

    Thank You for guiding my ship full of thoughts. I began focusing on the clock during my quiet time and You interrupted me as if to say, "Christina, you're on My watch. **Focus on My hands instead of the clock's hands.** I have given You exactly the amount of time <u>I</u> want so you can complete today's assignments. Only <u>I</u> can redeem time. Remember to honor My timetable. Come sit at My table and be filled with food for thought that will richly nourish you."

    Thank You, supernatural Spirit! Thank You for trusting me enough to hear You speak exactly what I needed to hear at that time! I love You, Father Time!

    I'm punching in <u>and</u> out on Your time clock,

Felicity

Lord,

    Thank You for my laptop and stand-up desk. With summer being here, I'm able to wheel the desk out to the patio to write when it's most light.

    I love the luxury of standing on healthy legs and grateful that I'm not confined to sitting in an office (or worse, being in an environment without windows). On rainy days, I can move the desk to face a window and celebrate Your washing our earth while I work.

    Thank You for guiding Tig to buy these gifts for me.

    Love,

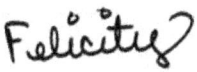

Christina M. Eder

Great Provider,

    Thank You for a conversation with a coworker. She asked, "What if tomorrow we got only what we said 'thank You' for today?" I consider myself pretty grateful, yet that question caused me to pause to think about specific praises I hadn't considered.

> **Make my life produce excellent return on Your priceless investment on the Cross.**

    I'd have a monumental list of detailed gratuities; so instead of writing thousands of praises, I head out for a walk to verbally speak these treasures from You. As we walk, lay on my heart the lessons You've taught and the blessin's You've showered.

    Help me appreciate Your correction because You care enough to invite me to adjust my will to Your will. Make my life produce excellent return on Your priceless investment on the Cross.

    Love,
    A daughter learning to gratefully surrender

Name Giver,

Thank You for a new prayer pattern. I have a friend Jeff and yesterday while I was praying for him, I began recalling other Jeffs I have known. I didn't have identifiable areas of prayer for each Jeff, but while their faces came to mind, I asked You to light and guide their path.

> **You know their full name, needs, desires, struggles and celebrations.**

I may only remember a person's first name and face, but You know their full name, needs, desires, struggles and celebrations. You are One Being with many names. I refer to You as Jesus, God, Dad, Father, Lord, Creator and Savior. Continue to guide my talk to You about Your people, with names You lay on my heart.

Love,

Christina Mae Maryann Mahr Eder (my parent-given name)

a.k.a. Felicity? (Your spiritual conversation name for me)

Christina M. Eder

Crafter of WOW moments!

Thank You! I'm at a park overlooking our city, watching the sun rise. Tig and I have hit a rough patch in our relationship, and I needed to walk to a higher elevation. I felt a nudge to walk counterclockwise toward the park. A few steps into my trek, I looked down and there was a BRIGHT SHINY NEW penny on the ground! It felt like a reminder that I need to direct my thoughts to go the opposite direction when my injured heart wants to go "south."

Your husband may be moon, You may be sun, but You share My sky!

I sat down at a picnic table in the direct sunlight and there was <u>another</u> penny on the round tabletop! It was as if the coin beckoned me with Your Spirit to say, "Sit at My table, go full circle and come back to My view about marriage.

Your husband may be moon, You may be sun, but You share My sky! Keep Your eyes fixed on the stars, planets and, most of all, Me, who is above ALL."

Thank You for more than 2¢ of wisdom. I get an abundant cash advance from Your golden treasure chest.

Learning to love,

Christina

Christina M. Eder

Thought Guider,

    Thank You for a chuckle and reality check during this morning's drive. I had a head full of unorganized thoughts and as I drove, my mind chatter was noisy. I reached for the radio knob to turn down its volume and realized I didn't even have the radio on! ☺

    Thank You for this comical correction. Help me redirect my station and tune in to Your regularly scheduled programs! Thank You for switching my channel from static to Your clear surround sound!

    Two ears, one sound mind with You as my Station Manager,

> I had a head full of unorganized thoughts and as I drove, my mind chatter was noisy.

C

Jesus,

Thank You for a unique thought that teaches me about the sweet and sour tastes of life. Our culture screams, "innovate," but freaks out when groceries are moved in the store.

We want change, yet squawk when change includes natural aging processes or inconvenience (according to us ☺). Meanwhile, my spirit dies and soul starves when I'm unwilling to resuscitate my spirit or allow You to feed my soul.

Help me to consistently honor Your guidelines. I know I'll fall short, but allow me to quickly get up to know Your truth in word <u>and</u> action. You are the greatest innovator and not limited by time. You don't fear transition.

Thank You for seeing me through all phases of Your transformation — the sweet and sour, the old and new Testaments in my growth cycle.

Love,

Felicity

Christina M. Eder

Jesus,

    Thank You for giving me a deeper level of understanding of You through a grieving friend. Her son died four days ago. I want her to know she can ask or call me with anything she needs. I want her to know I can be trusted with her happy <u>and</u> hellish parts of life. She may prefer to retreat in silence, to be with You only. I don't want her to think she owes me an explanation or that she can only reach out when she's in a better head space.

    In reflecting about what I want for her, I realize You desire our trust and communication. You want me to come to You with my hallelujahs and heartaches. **You handle all needs perfectly.** You see the entire picture. You understand everything about me, yet respect my free will. You are immediately available but won't force Your help until I'm ready.

    If I have this deeply powered love for her, there's no way I can comprehend the extent of Your love for me. Just thinking about that places me in a cross path between speechless and over-speaking!

    Love,
    Your daughter

Author of words,

Thank You for two fun discoveries to "cure" a funk. This morning I struggled with spending too much time in my head and too little time in my writing. I was delaying a gritty edit, so I grabbed one of my published books and began reading out loud. I opened the book to read the first page that I turned to. Hearing my voice speak uplifting logical thinking redirected my thoughts.

> **I struggled with spending too much time in my head and too little time in my writing.**

Later, I needed my thesaurus to find an alternative word for that same gritty edit piece. I was looking for different word for "remove." On my way to finding "remove," I turned to the page that offered synonyms for rainbow. It listed three substitutes for rainbow. You colorfully showed me I can use a thesaurus/dictionary to expand my vocabulary <u>and</u> redefine my thought pattern!

Thank You for Your dual solutions that unblocked written and unwritten barriers!

Love,

Felicity

Christina M. Eder

Teacher,

    Thank You for teaching me through a gift of hearing. I listened to a pastor talk about changing our minds to become more surrendered to Your plans. She frequently used words such as: <u>controlling</u> her behavior; <u>forcing</u> herself to do x or y; <u>crucifying</u> her flesh.

    Like this pastor, these words used to be part of my natural vocabulary. I used a "take-charge" approach to discipline myself. I was so set on getting it "right" with You that I grew a mindset that blocked Your flow of love.

    You are gently teaching me who I am and who I am becoming. Your discipline is consistent and sometimes tough, but it's not harsh and abrasive.

    Thank You for drawing me into Your pattern of mercy and justice. You've helped me shift my thinking to say, "I would like" rather than "I don't want." Thank You for this kinder style of surrender. (Humorously, what do You think about this reframed approach? "I would like dark chocolate almonds" rather than "I don't want a plain milk-chocolate bar"? ☺)

    Thank You for encouraging me to consider Your makeovers. I would like Your mercy. I don't want my actions to lead You to teach me justice! Kindly. Gently,

Christina

Christina M. Eder

Road Maker,

    Thank You for showing me ways to move through a writer's potential traffic jam. You guided me to listen to one song and write one line that spoke to me. You suggested reading one page of any book or magazine and choose a sentence that invited curiosity or piqued my interest. In doing this, I regained focus and momentum.

    Thank You for protecting me from literary traffic delays. Direct me toward a less blocked road that leads to a smoother spiritual commute.

    On my roadway to meet You face to face.

Love,

KNEE DEEP

Puzzle Maker and Solver,

    Thank You for a 1,000-piece puzzle that interlocked enough lessons to write an entire book. There are at least a dozen connections within this 20-minute time frame of sitting in front of this puzzle board.

> **I like to assemble the "absolutes" to frame the space I need.**

My thoughts sometimes resemble these 1,000 colorful cardboard pieces. My mind may look like this puzzle when I first opened the box. I've watched some people put puzzles together and they group colors together. Others frequently refer to the box for the puzzle's full picture. I prefer to secure the border pieces first. I like to assemble the "absolutes" to frame the space I need.

    I construct inner pieces in varying ways. Sometimes pieces fit together rapidly. Sometimes it takes a lot of patience to shape it. Whatever order or whatever pace, I complete the full picture one piece at a time.

    Like the hare and tortoise, slow and steady. Like Martha and Mary, listen and move. Consistent faithfulness. Even though I have about

Christina M. Eder

750 of the 1,000 pieces left to assemble on this puzzle, You remind me to stay the course.

A side pondering... If I could see my life in puzzle form, I wonder how many pieces I have completed so far on earth? What design, colors and scenery are You putting together? Please interlock my individual pieces so it resembles Your complete picture.

Intrigued but not puzzled,

Journalist of my Life,

    Thank You for reminding me that to uncover a story line, I need to ask who, what, where, when, how and why. I want to uncover – and be covered by – Your story. Please guide me to know who, what, where and when I am to move or wait. Guard me from thinking I need to know the how or why before I DO what You tell me.

    Keep my eyewitness slanted toward You. May my words only lead with Your truth. Thank You for these author's guidelines!

    Love,

    Felicity

Christina M. Eder

Jesus,

    Thank You for spiritual transportation to Your ICU (Inner Check-Up). I admit myself into Your hospital with a critical heart condition. This stems from a diet of self-discovery which has manifested into self-absorption.

    After decades of trying to be seen for the "real me," I want to respect the "real me" whom You've created. I've learned more about who You are and who I am in You. Sadly, instead of growing kinder and gentler, I've become more impatient and irritable. I'm agitated by surface-level conversations and stagnant living steeped in fear or blame.

    Help me be filled with patience for people as we develop at Your pace. Guard me from taking my recent lessons and lording them over others. I ask Your forgiveness (and a surgical removal of these unlovingly clogged arteries).

    Keep my heart beating in love!

    Love,
        Felicity

> **Help me be filled with patience for people as we develop at Your pace.**

Jesus,

Thank You for a painful, but necessary, reality check. In my quest to know, love and serve You, my wholehearted fervency has become cold-hearted rigidity!

I've become attracted to a freer way of living — and it causes my spirit to soar! I've inwardly flown to new heights with You, but outwardly dive bombed to new depths. How has this happened? To know and love You but not kindly serve Your people? What an oxymoron! (heavy on the moron ☺) The more I am with You, the less I want to be around people? Help me through this paradox!

Gratefully, I have been introduced to mindfulness and my eternal destination with present-moment mentality. Guard me against condemnation. Rescue me from condemning others. Help me send others forward with the same peace You do with me.

Christina M. Eder

    Remind me to know and love You first. Guide me to *act* upon that knowledge and love so I can lovingly serve Your Creation.

    Thank You for clearing today's path before I practice living with loving mindfulness. Head me toward Your eternal destination.

    Love,

    Felicity

Creator,

Thank You for a delicious way to creatively encourage someone's smile!

It's Monday and we had a dozen mini Kit Kats and Almond Joy bars left over from a weekend party. Instead of storing them in our cupboard, I wrote a message on a sticky note and attached it to each candy wrapper. On the Kit-Kats, I wrote, "Happy Monday! Give someone a break!" On the Almond Joy wrappers, I wrote, "It may be nutty, but I believe you'll find joy in your Monday!"

I've gotten to deliver two of the twelve so far. They're a perfect size to give a quick handoff to a neighbor, mail carrier, cashier or friend. Thank You for providing snacks from our weekend gathering <u>plus</u> having leftovers to leave with others!

Christina M. Eder

Spirit Guide,

Thank You for giving me a way to interact more like Jesus would have! Sometimes I'm in the throes of an impenetrable cold-hearted threatening rage for no reason. It lands hard with crashing waves of anger, seemingly out of nowhere.

While I was trying to release this bitter edginess, I pictured (friend). You know how she's grown through painful street cred. When I saw her in my mind's eye, I suddenly thought, "How would (name) respond to this battle?"

> **Sometimes I'm in the throes of an impenetrable cold-hearted threatening rage for no reason.**

You helped me recall other women who have mentored me through their character. You brought specific names and faces to mind and asked, "Would (name) accept my behavior?" "What would (name) say if she heard me say that?" How long would (name) allow me to rant?" "Would this make (name) proud of me?"

This unusual-to-me approach caused me to visualize women who kindly hold me accountable. By imagining their response to my thoughts or behaviors, You guided me back toward regaining Your smile!

From Felicity

in practice form for heaven (where there will be nothing bitter, nothing biting!)

Christina M. Eder

Jesus,

    Thank You for a desire and free spirit to travel. I've craved road trips and frequent outings. Financially, vacations aren't part of a present budget. While I wait in hope for You to opening roadways for exploring Your creation, You've hinted that You've mapped out changes and joyful destinations.

    Several women in my life have expressed an increased yearning for changes. They want a shake-up in their routine but remain stuck in their current mindset. You gave me the idea to reach out to them individually and invite them to take a small day trip. We could try a new-to-us restaurant or go to a shop that we've wanted to check out but never took the time (yet).

> **There are many mom-and-pop shops and small-town cafés opening after a surge of downtown renovation projects.**

    There are many mom-and-pop shops and small-town cafés opening after a surge of downtown renovation projects. If I invite one woman to join me for a short weekly field trip, I'd get 52 travel companions, 52 different conversations, 52 experiences with 52 destinations in one year. This would also support small communities and businesses by having two people patronizing their business rather than if I went solo.

Thank You for this oxygen pumped into my blood stream! I'm traveling lightly in the spirit just thinking of this possibility!

Love from Your creative explorer of Your world,

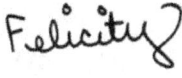

Christina M. Eder

Jesus,

    Thank You for a sweet recall that came from an interview question. I asked my interviewee about her greatest compliment. She shared a handwritten note in a Mother's Day card her son wrote as a child. This lady is all of 70 so throughout many years of compliments, her son's message ranks as her highest compliment.

    When I was writing her story, I thought about what my greatest compliment has been. My answer would be being voted as "Person with the Best Smile" in my high-school class. My smile. No words. No cost. No athletic prowess or academic showing. Simply a gift from You that 120+ classmates saw.

    I want to be perpetually remembered for using Your natural radiance to share genuine smiles with everyone. As long as I have <u>Your</u> vote, that's all I need to smile easily.

> **I want to be perpetually remembered for using Your natural radiance to share genuine smiles with everyone.**

From my pearly whites to Your pearly gates: a bridge between earth and heaven's waters,

Christina

Christina M. Eder

Jesus,

 Thank You for a reflection of Your crucifixion, Holy Saturday and Easter. As I think about my day, I experienced all three phases of Your death and life (thankfully not the crucifixion part but an inner flogging and thorns)! I had 16 hours of extremely painful barbs, periods of waiting and intense breakthrough. These 16 hours have felt like 16 days and I'm sitting in bed, absolutely spent.

 This visual gave me a way to picture a smidgen of what You endured in three days. You teach me through a cycle of Good Friday lessons, Holy Saturday waiting and Resurrected celebration. Thank You for this Easter message in June. Help me appreciate a blend of heartache, hopeful waiting and welcomed blessings. Inhale, pause, exhale!

 With renewal, at a crossroad. I'm seeking to walk in Your footpath.

 Love,

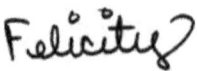

Lord,

    Thank You for a simplistic way to counter the world's harshness around our differences. You summarize by "saying" we all come from a woman's body and we will all die.

    Diverse cultures, assorted race, location, era, education, etc., but we're all created through You from one woman. There will be numerous causes of death, at varying ages and times, but physical death is how You choose to usher us out of this world.

> **We live colorfully and practice earthly life uniquely.**

    Keep me from assuming or judging. Help me celebrate Your creative variations. Guide me to respect all children of all ages. We live colorfully and practice earthly life uniquely. Until You unite us in the commonality of death, let us live in revealing peace,

Christina M. Eder

Lord Almighty,

    Thank You for a steady stream of revelation from the floodgates of Your teaching! I consider today as a day of spiritual eviction. I've been residing in pity, guilt, blame, defensiveness, fits of anger and self-traumatization for nearly five decades. (These ugly traits are not part of my 50-year golden anniversary party.☺)

    I need to use much scrap paper to write the repulsive parts of my heart (which filled more than six pages of gritty confession that are being withheld from publication).

    Thank You for stopping my thoughts here. I wanted to confess everything to You all at once. You jumped in, mid thought, to remind me You've been here through all I've experienced and will experience. Cleanse me from this sickbed, diseased by septic lies and self-serving motives.

    Lord, I write this personal declaration of independence so I can recall these transformational claims. I recognize I'll need to reference this frequently while I practice this metamorphosis.

    "I file suit against myself and file these documents (referring to my six confession pages)

> **I consider today as a day of spiritual eviction.**

with Your court. The selfish Christina has a long history of self-absorption. Expect this initial breakup to be painful. The foolish Christina has encountered pinnacles and pits. She will continue to do so. It'd be ridiculous to think her pain would automatically disappear. Allow her graceful tenacity to release the deed to this shack where her heart currently resides."

Creator, You've given me a vision with a capital V. It's outstanding and superior! Its impressiveness requires much more than I have. It's beyond what I see today. <u>Every</u> fiber in my DNA <u>needs</u> to follow this assignment. I willingly write and life coach, out of respectful obedience and joy for You, my Creator.

This Vision unites nearly all my relationships with Your future endeavors. Grant me abundance to patiently wait for You to align these pieces.

Court dismissed... I want to be expunged from past condemnation. I ask for complete renovation so I can live with a " 'Well done, good and faithful servant' ruling." Until then, keep me on Your judgment seat.

Order in the court. Signed, sealed and sent in love,

Felicity

Christina M. Eder

Creative Thinker,

Thank You for shedding light onto a sometimes-uncomfortable experience.

I have yet to hear someone say that seventh grade was their best year. Few people say that their confidence peaked at 12 or 13 years old!

I jokingly say I've traveled more than 50 revolutions around the sun and each year brings more acceptance that my life resembles a series of seventh-grade awkward moments. (Who knows, maybe this letter to You may become one of my stand-up comedy skits. ☺)

In a sense, all Your children are seventh graders on earth's practice field toward our eternal game of Destiny. I have yet to hear someone say that seventh grade was their best year. Few people say that their confidence peaked at 12 or 13 years old!

Thinking back to my seventh-grade year, I'm nearly re-traumatized. In Your Word, You teach me we're all beautifully and wonderfully made. You created us worthy, but as a 12-year-old, I felt anything but worthy. My <u>self</u>-worth was based on my<u>self</u>.

In recalling a seventh grade I've tried to repress, I wanted to fit in; wanted to be noticed, while at the same time wishing I could shrink behind someone or something. My body felt mismatched, my emotions wrecked havoc. I thought everyone was looking at me. I was lonely, defined myself as ugly and the list goes on. I wondered whether I could trust <u>any</u>one.

I've come to learn that <u>You</u> notice me. I'm <u>not</u> alone. Your group membership matters most. You invite me to Your parties, projects and sleepovers. Still, my inner seventh grader wonders and wanders in this classroom called life. My teachers, classmates, location and books may be different now, yet the lessons and tests continue.

In this ever-changing mind, heart, body and spirit, You remain consistent. I've grown to trust You. You've given me a sound mind, a healthily formed body. You listen to my questions and patiently teach. I love You for accepting and developing and transforming me.

Thank You for guiding my studies toward a heavenly graduation. I imagine You calling me to the head of the class to hand me a diploma

that reads, "Well done, good and faithful servant."
   Until then, I'm Your series of seventh-grade show-and-tell witness,

Lord,

    Thank You for deploying me as one of Your soldiers for this earthly mission. I began my spiritual training as a "grunt" with whopping ideas. I was armed with unfounded wisdom, ready to fight, to be promoted among the ranks.

> **I was armed with unfounded wisdom, ready to fight, to be promoted among the ranks.**

    It has taken me nearly five decades under Your command to realize I am not an army of one. I am under one God, yet I frequently draw my gun as a solo troop. While the United States prepares to celebrate this 4th of July, focus our attention on freedom. Freedom in You only, <u>one</u> nation under <u>God</u>!

    Protect me from misfiring bullets loaded with self-made reliance. Guide me to declare my dependence on You. Rule over and light my path so I live in subordination to You!

    I hold my right hand over my heart, pledging to be united with and for You. I'm

Christina M. Eder

grateful to defend Jesus. While He was a soldier on earth, He shed all his blood fighting for You.

Love, Your humble and free servant,

C

Lord,

Thank You for Your grounding! In a panic, I reached out to ask others to pray about what happened to Tig in the garage. You quickly guided me to go to Your throne before the phone. Please use my shaky hand to write these scattered thoughts while I talk to You about this situation.

> **Guide me to understand that his process of handling emergencies is different from mine but as long as we're both leaning on *You*, that's the right way.**

Tig was backing up his car hauler and one of his shop dog-buddies ran behind him and got hit. The dog is lying under the hauler so he's out of Tig's reach to move him. Thankfully, he's not pinned under the hauler! Because it's the Fourth of July, Tig can't reach any shelters, and the police are significantly delayed.

I'm forcing myself to sit still to concentrate on writing calmness into myself and Tig. I know it's best to be still in a storm rather than throw combustible material into the wind. You're calling me to trust You while You work out this potentially fatal situation. You care about all Your creation, including furry beings.

Thank You for drawing me to read <u>The Power of a Praying Wife</u> (ironically, written by <u>Stormie</u> Omartian!) Prepare us for whatever lies ahead regarding this severely injured dog.

Help me support Tig *however* he needs. Guide me to understand that his process of handling emergencies is different from mine but as long as we're both leaning on <u>You</u>, that's the right way.

Please don't let this dog endure prolonged suffering. Prepare me as a wife to be steady for Tig. Pour Your peaceful balm over our wounds. Thank You for Your mercy over this dog. Grant Tig and all potential helpers the clear guidance they need to minister to this dog.

With hurt. With love. With wobbly trust,

Gentle Shepherd,

    Thank You for helping me discover a gentle self-care treatment. It's been humid and I used a cotton ball to absorb my facial oil and smudged eye makeup. As I rubbed that soft cotton across my face, I was surprised how quickly I felt soothed and energized.

    That 30-second move inspired me to leave a cotton ball on my bathroom vanity to remind myself to be gentle. I need calm so I can share Your peacefulness with others.

    Treading softly under Your hand,

C

Christina M. Eder

Lord,

    Thank You for teaching me that a lull can be Your reminder to "Be Still" and *know* that You are God. Help me not confuse a lull of complacency with a lull of restoration that renews my soul.

    Love,

    C

Ruler of the Universe,

Thank You for re-aligning my priorities and boundaries. In the publishing and marketing world, "creating a presence" is a buzz phrase. I've allowed this hype to become habitual. During my hourly check-in walk with You, You showed me that an online presence doesn't mean an online predominance (a.k.a., an idol that distracts me from following Your calling on my life: to write, to life coach!)

> **You showed me that an online presence doesn't mean an online predominance.**

You graciously reminded me that <u>You</u> know my presence. You "like me" on Your Facebook. You give me rave reviews simply because I'm one of Your followers. In Your social media, You love, care and support me. You have unlimited stars, a crown of jewels and glory in heaven.

Thank You for Your faithfulness, on earth and heaven. I'm humbled and speechless in Your presence,

XO

Christina

Christina M. Eder

Jesus,

Thank You for a natural curiosity. My journalism teacher taught that to be a great writer, you needed to develop an eye like a camera, to look for various angles, lighting and interaction.

I have an 80-something-year-old neighbor who straps his binoculars around his neck whenever he goes for a walk. He walks a similar route several times a day, but despite his frequently traveled roads, he models what Mrs. P. taught in my journalism class.

He said he stays alert by being a perpetual tourist.

Yesterday we crossed paths and I jokingly pointed to his binoculars and asked him if he was out bird watching. He said he stays alert by being a perpetual tourist. He shared this wisdom: "a local tourist. That's essentially an oxymoron because wherever we are on God's earth, we are local. This minute, this day, these circumstances, this season is the first time any of us have experienced life. Therefore, we are all tourists in a foreign land."

When he saw my wide-eyed, speechless response, my neighbor quickly disengaged from our conversation, pointed to his binoculars and said he needed to hurry off to capture more of the local sights.

Thank You for this fun, insightful tourist stop on Your earth. Final destination? Heaven! All aboard!

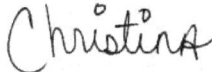

Christina M. Eder

Lord,

    Thank You for redirecting my energy. In a desire to do Your will, I have become so focused on <u>finding</u> it that I've missed opportunities to <u>follow</u> it.

    Jesus, thank You for living an example that follows God one footprint at a time. Putting Your step ahead of mine, lead me to align it with Your imprint! Thank You for tying a big shoelace message into a tiny knot of time.

☺ Felicity

Wow! Lord!

    Thank You for Your strong movement! You exposed a connection through a technological lesson. I've used the computer less and You've used my "off screen" time to keep me tuned in more frequently to Your network!

I've used the computer less and You've used my "off screen" time to keep me tuned in more frequently to Your network!

    There are surges of examples I could list here, but it may overload a circuit breaker ☺. You've created non-computer, non-screen opportunities. I see how many free choices I've been taking for granted.

    If I didn't live in this country, this era, at this time, in this community, these choices wouldn't even be a dream, much less an option.

    On this Independence Day, I wave my flag to surrender and honor You. I shout Your victory cry over death. Thank You for inner birth that required a death to self.

 XO

Christina M. Eder

To my Great Conversationalist,

Thank You for crossing my path with a friend. Today, she stopped me to chat about something her fourth-grade teacher taught. That teacher challenged her to remove the phrase "I can't do this" and replace it with "I can get through this."

Nearly six decades have passed since Joyce's teacher encouraged her through that short message, but it stuck with her. I think about these valuable one-line nuggets provide gold blocks of light.

As I walked away, I thought about reframing my approach. I will say, "Maybe I can't do x, y, or z <u>now</u>, but I <u>will</u> discover something from it."

Provider,

    Thank You for a workshop idea to teach about tithing. You ask us to give 10 percent of our gross income toward kingdom investments. Considering You already own 100 percent of resources, it's ironic how bent out of shape we get when it comes to "our" money.

    I've seen rumpled fast-food wrappers strewn on the ground that resemble dollar bills. Unlike those fast-food wrappers, because of what money represents, this dirty green paper keeps people from littering the streets with it.

> **We are called to be generous. Guard me from fear of giving. Nobody can outgive You.**

    I'd like to call my workshop: "Faithful Generosity: A Test of a Dime." I'm thinking of handing workshop participants one dime when they entrance and one dime at their exit. Two dimes symbolize provision coming and going. I'm going to invite participants to keep one and give one away. I'm also going to challenge them to give freely, without wondering how the recipient will spend "their" dime.

Christina M. Eder

    Thank You for providing and trusting us to use Your resources wisely. We are called to be generous. Guard me from fear of giving. Nobody can outgive You.

    Thank You for giving 100 percent. Thank You that You request only 10 percent of our dirty green paper.

    With invested trust,

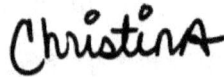

Lord,

 Thank You for some sprinkled comic relief today... I wore white pants and realized how uptight I've been all day. I've been cautious about spilling, sitting down, brushing up against something.

 As simple as this is, thank You for gently telling my spirit, "If a pair of pants is stealing your joy, give yourself some 'goodwill' and donate them."

 When I change out of my clothes tonight, tomorrow's errands will include a trip to the donation center. Thanks!

 Clothed in white purity ☺

Christina M. Eder

Laughter Giver,

    Thank You for my getting to witness a store employee who found something so funny that she snorted when she laughed. I have no clue about what tickled her funny bone. I realized how foreign a belly laugh sounded. As the woman horse-cackled, her roar was a heavenly sound.

    Smiling out loud,

    Felicity

Lord,

Thank You for how You're developing me as a transitional life coach. When I first began coaching, I used my academy training to bring a list of at least six to 10 "power questions." I knew I didn't need to ask all those questions, but I feared conversational lulls. When a client would respond, "I don't know," I'd panic. I've learned to respect their "I don't know" answer as meaning they don't know, as of <u>now</u>.

> **I don't know all the answers and that's okay.**

By using this slower pace and pausing, I have learned about trusting You for answers while they reflect. I believe these clients have answers somewhere in them. They might not grasp them now, but the answers are there. I need to carry my belief in clients' processing answers to my own trust that Your wisdom will manifest in me.

I don't know all the answers and that's okay. You'll reveal them as I need them (not always when I want them ☺)

Christina M. Eder

Natural Transformer,

Thank You for Your guidance during an appointment when a client came to our life-coaching session in a funk. We were doing a phone session and her downtrodden tone lingered in her voice.

> **She saw colors, touched leaves, heard worker sounds and smelled freshly cut grass. She could "taste" autumn in the air.**

When she stopped talking, I asked, "Can we stop our session and do something I haven't tried before?"

Thankfully, she said yes.

So I asked her to take time to thoughtfully observe her surroundings.

After our two-minute timeout, I asked her to engage every one of her senses and verbally detail her environment one sense at a time. She saw colors, touched leaves, heard worker sounds and smelled freshly cut grass. She could "taste" autumn in the air. After her sensory description, we continued our coaching session with fresh perception.

In that two-minute virtual nature walk, she gained traction over her rocky start. We finished with one of our best coaching sessions so far!

Thank You for this spur-of-the-moment, out-of-the-box method to gently encourage light that replaced heavy energy.

Love from Your daughter surrounded by Your natural upgrades,

Christina M. Eder

Jesus,

    Thank You for Your discernment between contemplation and rumination. Whenever I'm tempted to over think or over articulate, You recommended getting one sheet of scrap paper to write my thoughts in rough-draft format.

    Writing slows my thinking because I need more time to process thoughts to paper. I found that when I see my thoughts through handwriting, I can stop the cycle of overthinking. It's good to think. It can become dangerous to overthink ☺

    Fewer words from me, more power to You!

    Love,

Jesus,

Thank You for reminding me loyal friendship doesn't mean continual communication. Consistency doesn't equal frequency. Sometimes a gradual trickle is more appreciated than a few floods of connection.

Some people have a natural ebb and flow in maintaining friendships. They are energized by significant interaction. I require considerable space and prefer one-on-one short visits. Help me respect natural boundaries. Teach me to accept myself as a faithful friend who needs space and time to process. I know You understand what that means through Your spirit!

Love to my provider, sustainer, encourager, savior and forever loyal friend!

Teach me to accept myself as a faithful friend who needs space and time to process.

Christina M. Eder

My Heavenly Father,

    I have more than a half century of earthly experience with You. My parents taught me the prayer Jesus taught His disciples. After thousands of "Our Father" recitations, sometimes His words become rote. I repeat them from memory, but sometimes not from heart.

    Last week, when I heard someone speak about "them" and "they," I realized I was one of the "them" and the "they" she referred to! Thud! Initially I became defensive from her generalized assumption. Later, I relied on the familiar "Our Father" to ask You to release my defensiveness from her glib comment.

    The well-known prayer grounded me from becoming entangled with my ego weeds. I quickly

> After thousands of "Our Father" recitations, sometimes His words become rote. I repeat them from memory, but sometimes not from heart.

blurted out "Our Father, who are in heaven, hallowed be Thy..." When I got to "on earth as it is in heaven," I slowed my pace.

What happens in my spirit if I substitute "us" for "me?" To replace "we" with "I"? And "me" for "we"? To say, "Forgive <u>me</u> <u>my</u> debts as <u>I</u> forgive others who trespass against <u>me</u> and lead <u>me</u> not into temptation but deliver <u>me</u> from the evil one."

Brilliant! The source of my frustration about this woman's judgment became foundational. When I personalize what these words mean, You get my attention. It penetrates my heart. I'm immediately practicing Your guidance, for the benefit of "them" (which includes me ☺). I love my Father Who is in heaven.

From one Your children toddling from a literary lily pad,

Christina M. Eder

Lord,

Thank You for guiding my attention to read a vehicle's window sticker that led to prayer. The sticker said, "Lord, Your heavenly angel wings were ready to receive Papaw, but my heart wasn't ready to let him go."

To me, this raw honesty says, "I'm in pain but I believe." The driver's heart may have been stuck, but nonetheless, he drove forward.

Thank You for reminding me of an insightful answer from the long-asked question, "How can a good God allow bad things happen?" The wise sage replied, "God is not responsible for hate in the world. He creates in love. He will not and cannot be expected to get credit or blame for consumer abuse."

Bless this family and their journey and tedious process of grief,

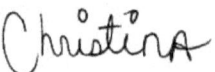

7-16-20

Lord,

    Thank You for ends and beginnings. Today completes this adventure of what I call my Zowie project. You've read my handwritten letters from October 20 to today, July 16. These dates mark our son's conception-to-birth period. I know this book will be called **KNEE DEEP**. **You've watched me grow through trial and error, through wins and whines.** You'll use my vulnerability to show how You've been with me, not only for these past nine months, but all time before and after this assignment.

    I have more questions than answers. What will be my next step when I review these four enormous stacks of written scrap-paper letters to You? I remained faithful in handwriting these pieces without editing or critiquing. I kept them in chronological order and haven't read them since the day I wrote them.

    For next week, I've rented the Dorothy Day cottage at Penule Ridge Retreat Center and will bring the accordion file stuffed with my handwritten heart. I'm equally nervous and curious of

Christina M. Eder

what I'll read from this nine-month literary recap. I anticipate this reflection to be like paging through a penned scrapbook or photo album.

    Guide me in this process. Help me be open. Move me to allow You to govern all aspects of whatever <u>KNEE DEEP</u> is to be. You've watched me grow through trial and error, through wins and whines. I'm not the same person I was nine months ago.

    With curious nerves, trusting in peaceful resolution that will follow because of You,

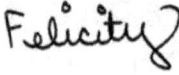

7-18-20

Lord Almighty, Literary Master,

 Whoo FROGGIE! It's Saturday, two days after I finished what I think will become book #3 in the FROG series, <u>KNEE DEEP</u>. The second FROG Blog book, <u>UNTHAWED: Lessons from a Frozen Lily Pad</u>, was published yesterday – one day after I completed Your nine-month assignment.

 Meanwhile, I'm preparing the team for <u>Tadpoles</u>, a children's anthology of FROG blog. will follow <u>Poetry Pod</u> (according to my plan on this day).

> **I have deep fulfillment in knowing I completed this assignment as purely as I knew how.**

 Father, help me not to become trapped in a swamp of entangled weeds. Guard me from distractions out of fear of having this book printed. It'll be under Your guidance and I know only You could have called me to share some of our paper chats.

 I have countless unanswered questions, yet I'm grateful for this peaceful sense of surrender. I have temperance (at this moment) in knowing these assignments will be written through You and

Your process. During this nine-month written journey, You've held my hand. You've guided my penned words. As Paul wrote, I have learned to be satisfied and remain joyful.

Fortunately, I'm in a head space (right now) to write this truth. I will witness storms because of an act of God, but You will protect me. I ponder these nine months of writing from an innocent voice, like the one I used as a third grader scribing my burgundy diary pages.

I'd thought I would finish with a sense of completion. I felt I'd have a sense of conclusion on July 16. Instead, I have little resolution. I do have a contented detachment. I have deep fulfillment in knowing I completed this assignment as purely as I knew how.

During this "zowie" adventure, You gave me a new lease on life. It's a vision with a capital V. There are further details than what I'll write here, but I choose these pieces to record as somewhat of a time capsule. I envision these are a few of next steps for me. I write my ideas in pencil. Please write Your details in pen (or engrave them in stone? ☺):

- ♥ Donate a portion of the book and speaking-engagement proceeds to small non-profits.

- Create opportunities to tutor new authors and mentor young ladies (especially 18- to 30-year-olds).
- Increase phone-coaching clients, especially those experiencing grief, terminal illness or hospice.
- Find a producer for what You've given me to develop through podcasts, stand-up comedy and YouTube teaching.
- Travel frequently.
- Eliminate all debt (vehicles, land, grudges, unforgiveness and all habits that don't serve You).
- Write a weekly column for newspapers and/or magazines.
- Build a small chapel to house Your and my Martha and Mary Writing Studio and life-coaching office.
- Keep my cast of characters diverse. Remind me that one or two people cannot fulfill my earthly dreams or disappointments.
- Send everyone and everything in love.

Where do I go from here? You know. You're already there. Grant me trust to follow Your lead. Give me strength to walk by Your

Christina M. Eder

side. You've already taken the leap. Hold my hand as I take a step, one at a time.

    With love,
    Your daughter Christina
    spiritually rebirthed as Felicity :)

KNEE DEEP

Christina M. Eder

I THIRST
By Saint Mother Teresa

Dearest, it is true. I stand at the door of your heart, day and night. Even when you are not listening, even when you doubt it could be Me, I am there. I await even the smallest sign of your response, even the least whispered invitation that will allow Me to enter.

I come with My mercy, with My desire to forgive and heal you, and with a love for you beyond your comprehension ~ a love every bit as great as the love I have received from the Father...

And I want you to know that whenever you invite Me, I do come ~ always, without fail. Silent and unseen I come, but with infinite power and love, and bringing the many gifts of my Spirit. I come with My mercy, with My desire to forgive and heal you, and with a love for you beyond your comprehension ~ a love every bit as great as the love I have received from the Father... "As much as the Father has loved me, I have love you" (John 15:10). I come ~ longing to console you and give you strength, to lift you up and bind all your wounds. I bring you My light, to dispel your darkness and all your doubts. I come with My power, that I might carry you and all your burdens; with My grace, to touch your heart and transform your life and My peace I give to still your soul.

    I know you, Dearest, through and through. I know everything about you. The very hairs of your head I have numbered. Nothing in your life is unimportant to Me. I have followed you through the years, and I have loved you always ~ even in your wanderings. I know every one of your problems. I know your needs and worries. And yes, I know all your sins. But I tell you again, I love you ~ not for what you have done or haven't done ~ I love you for you, for the beauty and dignity My Father gave you by creating you in His own dignity and image. It is a dignity you have often forgotten, a beauty you have tarnished by sin. But I love you as you are, and I have shed My blood to win you back. If you only ask Me with faith, My grace will touch all that needs changing in your life, and I will give you the strength to free yourself from sin and all its destructive power.

    I know what is in your heart ~ I know your loneliness and all your hurts ~ the rejections, the judgments, the humiliations, I carried it all before you. And I carried it all for you, so you might share My strength and victory. I know especially your need for love ~ how you are thirsting to be loved and cherished. But how often have you thirsted in vain, by seeking that love selfishly, striving to fill the emptiness inside you with passing pleasures ~ with the even greater emptiness of sin. Do you thirst for love? "Come to me all you who thirst..." (John 7:37). I will satisfy and fill you. Do you thirst to be cherished? I cherish you more than you can imagine ~ to the point of dying on a cross for you.

    I thirst for you. Yes, that is the only way to even begin to describe My love for you. I THIRST FOR YOU. I thirst to love you and to be loved by you ~ that is how precious you are to Me. I THIRST FOR YOU. Come to Me, and I will fill your heart and heal your wounds. I will make you a new creation, and give you peace, even in all your trials. I THIRST FOR YOU. You must never doubt My mercy, My acceptance of you, My desire to forgive, My longing to bless you and live My life in you. I THIRST FOR YOU. If you feel unimportant in the eyes of the world, that matters not at all. For Me, there is no one any more important in the entire world than you. I THIRST FOR YOU. Open to Me, come to Me, thirst for Me, give Me your life ~ and I will prove to you how important you are to My heart.

    Don't you realize that My Father already has a perfect plan to transform your life, beginning from this moment? Trust in Me. Ask Me every day to enter and take charge of your life ~ and I will. I promise you before My Father in heaven that I will work miracles in your life. Why would I do this? Because I THIRST FOR YOU. All I ask of you is that you entrust yourself to Me completely. I will do all the rest.

    Even now I behold the place My Father has prepared for you in My kingdom. Remember that you are a pilgrim in this life, on a journey home. Sin can never satisfy you or bring you the peace you seek. All that you have sought outside of Me has only left you more empty so do not cling to the things of this life. Above all, do not run from Me when you fall. Come to Me without delay. When you give Me your sins, you give Me the joy of being your Savior. There is nothing I cannot forgive and heal so come now and unburden your soul.

> *You forget Me, and yet I am seeking you every moment of the day...*

No matter how far you may wander, no matter how often you forget Me, no matter how many crosses you may bear in this life, there is one thing I always want you to remember, one thing that will never change. I THIRST FOR YOU ~ just as you are. You don't need to change to believe in My love, for it will be your belief in Me, in My love, that will change you. You forget Me, and yet I am seeking you every moment of the day ~ standing at the door of your heart and knocking. Do you find this hard to believe? Then look at the cross, look at My heart that was pierced for you. Have you not understood My cross? Then listen again to the words I spoke there ~ for they tell you clearly why I endured all this for you. "I THIRST" (John 19:28). Yes, I thirst for you ~ as the rest of the psalm verse I was praying says of Me: "I looked for love, and I found none" (Psalm 69:20). All your life I have been looking for your love ~ I have never stopped seeking to love you and be loved by you. You have tried many other things in your search for happiness; why not try opening your heart to Me, right now, more than you ever have before.

    Whenever you do open the door of your heart, whenever you come close enough, you will hear Me say to you again and again, not in mere human words but in spirit: No matter what you have done, I love you for your own sake. Come to me with your misery and your sins, with your troubles and needs, and with all your longing to be loved. I stand at the door of your heart and knock. Open to Me, for I THIRST FOR YOU, Dearest.

About the Author

Christina's life work includes teacher, writing tutor, and word crafter. She enjoys baking, crocheting, walking outdoors and handwriting cards. Christina has a creative approach to life that invites people to laugh, cry and explore with her. Sometimes people wonder about her, but she is genuine and true to her word.

Knee Deep: A 9-Month Whirlpool of Handwritten Letters to the Creator is book #3 in the FROG Blog series. She wrote her first book, *"Life's too Short for Dull Razors, Cheap Pens, and Worn-Out Underwear,"* to satisfy a long-term best friend's double dare. That "one-and-done gag" evolved into at least five subsequent books. Christina writes in short segments, to be read as stand-alone pieces or as part of a collection.

Christina M. Eder

Thank You From Christina

I wish all readers could meet Rita Reali and Red Paint Spilman. If you knew them, I could stop my tribute here because you would be able to identify their hearts with generous integrity, understanding, kindness and contagious spirit. They have an incredible pulse on how I process their feedback. They grasp and accept the way I show up for life is "so like Christina."

Rita and Red Paint have individual expertise and combine their professional talent to craft unique flairs for the FROG Blog series. As editor, Rita graciously knows how to gently nudge me, while non-judgmentally accepting my weaknesses. Red Paint, cover designer and accountability partner, has creativity oozing from his pores. He colorfully brushes designs (and overall life) with flexibility. Kudos for his confidence to present dynamic options while patiently respecting "my Christina-isms."

I'd exceed my word count or wear out a thesaurus if I continued listing their powerful impact. They paint value not only to my world, but, I believe, into our world in general. This is where I must remind myself to "Hush before I gush." So I'll follow my own advice and end my accolades for Rita Reali and Red Paint Spilman here.

Humbly, eternally grateful to these two powerful partners,

www.ingramcontent.com/pod-product-compliance
Lightning Source LLC
Chambersburg PA
CBHW071952070526
44583CB00015B/1157